Please Pray For Us

Please Pray For Us

JOHAN COMPANJEN

GENERAL EDITOR

Research by Justin Long

BETHANYHOUSE

Minneapolis, Minnesota

Published by Bethany House Publishers
A Ministry of Bethany Fellowship International
11400 Hampshire Avenue South
Bloomington, Minnesota 55438
www.bethanyhouse.com

Printed in the United States of America by
Bethany Press International, Bloomington, Minnesota 55438

Library of Congress Cataloging-in-Publication Data

Companjen, Johan.
    Please pray for us : praying for persecuted Christians in 52 nations / by Johan Companjen.
      p. cm.
    ISBN 0-7642-2416-6
    1. Persecution—Prayer-books and devotions—English. I. Title.
BR1602 .C65 2000
272'.9'090511—dc21

                                      00-009992

ABOUT THE CONTRIBUTORS

JOHAN COMPANJEN, general editor of *Please Pray for Us*, is president of Open Doors International (founded by Brother Andrew), which has served the Persecuted Church worldwide for forty-five years.

In 1967, at twenty-one years of age, Johan joined his countryman, Brother Andrew, in the unique work of Open Doors—even risking his life and freedom to serve the Persecuted Church worldwide. Johan's three-year missionary service in Vietnam was abruptly aborted in 1975 when he and his wife, Anneke, were evacuated prior to the fall of Saigon. For nearly 30 years, Johan worked alongside Brother Andrew as Communism's grip reached from Eastern Europe to China, Africa, and Latin America. With the fall of the Iron Curtain, Open Doors began a new focus on Christian persecution as it increasingly came to light throughout the Muslim world.

Consulting with church and ministry leaders worldwide, Johan spearheads Open Doors' global strategic plans to distribute Bibles and other materials in restricted countries. He prays with and encourages persecuted believers when he visits these dangerous areas.

Through this service, Johan has acquired extensive firsthand knowledge of the church in many countries around the world. His recognized expertise on the Persecuted Church makes him a sought-after speaker in gatherings from house churches to international conferences. As president of Open Doors International, Johan coordinates ministry offices in twenty-four countries with over two hundred full-time workers and thousands of volunteers.

Through years of personal experience, Johan knows that God opens doors for the gospel, which no man can shut, even in the world's most restricted areas. And today he continues the work begun in 1955 by Brother Andrew and proclaimed clearly in Revelation 3:2 to "strengthen that which remains and is on the point of death."

JUSTIN LONG, researcher, has been involved in missions trend research and analysis for nearly a decade. He is an associate editor of the *World Christian Encyclopedia* (2nd ed.) and has served as the managing editor of the AD2025 Global Monitor. He is presently responsible for a series of Web sites developed by the Network for Strategic Missions, including strategicnetwork.org, an online community of Christians serving unreached peoples and countries, and the Monday Morning Reality Check, a weekly editorial on the implications of mission trends, delivered via email (reality-check@egroups.com). He lives in Chesapeake, Virginia, with his wife Heidi and two children.

CONTENTS

INTRODUCTION

Prayer changes things. This is a central tenet of *Please Pray for Us* and the principle reason why it has been written. To our way of thinking, there are few Christian issues in greater need of prayer than the plight of the Persecuted Church.

At the turn of the millennium, nearly half of the world's countries experienced some level of persecution, more than fifty of them sharp to severe. These countries are home to over three billion people, more than half of the world's population. They deny freedom of religion, in most cases restrict or deny freedom to evangelize, and some go so far as to harass, arrest, imprison, torture, and even execute Christians. The worst cases are, for all intents and purposes, at war with Christianity.

In this prayer guide, fifty-two countries are presented alphabetically for your prayers—one for each week. With each we present a description of the nation and paragraphs regarding church life, persecution, the future, and prayer topics. The statistical box will give you a quick overview of the country; its data are derived from a variety of authoritative sources including population information from the United Nations, reports from Open Doors field offices, and material from published missiological research (notably *Operation World* and the *World Christian Encyclopedia*). All of the data presented are order-of-magnitude estimates and should not be used as exact figures. Under "Christians" in the statistical box, we give an indicator of the growth, or decline, of the church in terms of the population as a whole; e.g., the church may be adding members yet not rapidly enough to increase its share of the population, in which case we label it as "share declining."

Under "Church Life," a short history of the church in the nation is presented along with a few brief descriptions about what modern life is like for Christians in the country. Under "Persecution," the current state of restriction and persecution within the country is described in more detail, and in some cases stories

9

are included from members of the Persecuted Church in that country. Also, we list the probable future of Christianity within the nation, based on current trends, under the heading "The Future."

The paragraph telling of future expectations emphasizes the need for prayer. It is a statement of the *probable* future—but not necessarily of the *most desirable* one. Usually, it is the least desirable future of all. Unfortunately, secular activity has, so far, failed to stop religious persecution. Neither United Nations' resolutions, nor international efforts, have been able to open up these countries to religious freedom. If the most powerful nations on earth have failed to accomplish this, what can be done to change the future of these countries?

It should be remembered that, in general, persecution is not as severe today as it was under other world powers. Missiologists estimate that 175,000 lose their lives because of their faith each year, yet under the Roman Empire the rate of martyrdom was much more intense, and under some oppressors (e.g., Genghis Khan and Tamerlane) it has been catastrophic. Although more people died for their faith in the last century than in all the previous centuries combined, these numbers are due to the fact that the church is larger today, encompassing hundreds of millions of people.

The current rate of persecution actually represents a decline. With the fall of the Soviet Union, the average rate, according to missiologists, has been cut nearly in half. Satan's forces are hard at work against the church, but the victory of the church through Christ Jesus is assured. Already our world has seen divine breakthroughs, and we know the best is yet to come. One day our Lord will wipe away every tear.

Between now and then, we work in anticipation of His promise by wiping away as many tears as we can, by standing with our brothers and sisters, bearing their burdens, and helping to build the church. We trust that you, in prayer, will join us in this endeavor.

THE 52 COUNTRIES WHERE
FAITH COUNTS MOST

This list indicates the fifty-two countries in which persecution against Christians is currently the greatest—the countries where faith counts most. The countries are ranked according to the intensity of persecution.

1. Saudi Arabia
2. Sudan
3. Somalia
4. Yemen
5. North Korea
6. China
7. Laos
8. Vietnam
9. Iran
10. Morocco
11. Afghanistan
12. Maldives
13. Qatar
14. Libya
15. Comoro Islands
16. Egypt
17. Uzbekistan
18. Mauritania
19. Algeria
20. Djibouti
21. Turkmenistan
22. Brunei
23. Tunisia
24. Bhutan
25. Pakistan
26. Azerbaijan
27. Chiapas, Mexico
28. Oman
29. Colombia
30. Bahrain
31. Cuba
32. Kuwait
33. India
34. Indonesia
35. Nigeria
36. Myanmar
37. Turkey
38. Ethiopia
39. Chad
40. Cambodia
41. Tajikistan
42. Philippines
43. Nepal
44. Peru
45. Iraq
46. Malaysia
47. Bangladesh
48. Russia
49. Syria
50. Sri Lanka
51. Jordan
52. Israel

A GLOBAL TOUR

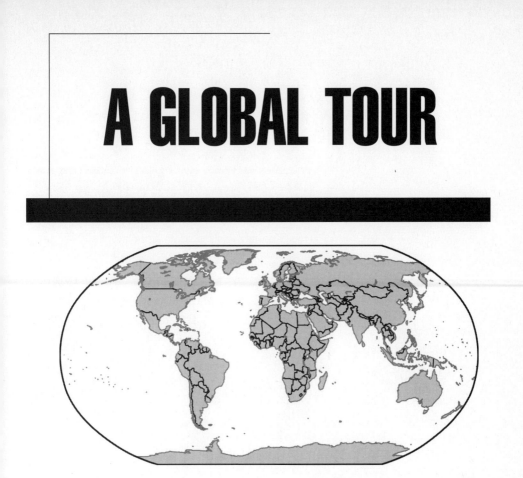

Please Pray for the Persecuted Church in:

AFGHANISTAN

Afghanistan has been in many ways defined by its location and its terrain. It has been called the "crossroads of Central Asia" because the legendary Khyber Pass on its eastern border with Pakistan is a strategic link between India and points west. Numerous world emperors have invaded Afghanistan in order to control this gateway, and most have failed in the end. The primary reason is that Afghanistan is cut virtually in two by the rugged mountains of the Hindu Kush, which form a natural hiding place and also a barrier to invading armies. The freedom fighters of every age had only to melt back into these mountains and wait for the opportune moments to strike at their captors. At the same time, the mountains of the Hindu Kush have enabled a nearly endless civil war between the government and whatever force—fundamentalist or liberal—has happened to be in opposition to it at the time, and they have also kept out modernizing influences (like technology), as well as the gospel.

The largest ethnic group is the Pashto (or Pashtun, Pathan), which makes up about one-third of the population. Tajiks make up a quarter, and other important minorities include the Uzbeks and the Hazara. Of the 22.7 million, 43 percent are under the age of fifteen and 80 percent live in rural areas.

Afghanistan has been fought over by empires ranging from Alexander the Great to the British. Most recently, an autocratic monarchy was overthrown (1973).

Republican rule was ended in a pro-Marxist coup in 1978, coupled with an invasion by Soviet forces. The armed conflict was a disaster for the country, finally leading to the withdrawal of Soviet forces in 1988–89 and the fall of the Communist regime in 1992. Disunity among the guerrillas then degenerated into civil war. In the past few years a military coalition called the Taliban has successfully gained control of 95 percent of the country. It is staunchly Islamic and enforces a rigid interpretation of *shari'a* law. In the course of the conflict, the economy has been completely crushed by nearly two decades of war. The countryside has been poisoned, bombed, and mined; half the housing, most of the complex irrigation systems, and a high proportion of the livestock, have been destroyed. Most of Afghanistan's workers are involved in agrarian jobs, with the most lucrative crop being opium. Many of the intellectuals abandoned the country after the Taliban took over.

The nation is 99 percent Muslim, 90 percent of whom are Sunnis. There are other small religious minorities, including a handful of Christians, most of whom are expatriates. Shi'as have been systematically persecuted during the takeover of the Taliban.

CHURCH LIFE

Christianity came to Afghanistan in the first centuries after Christ, and by A.D. 400 a bishop of Herat had been installed. Christianity was eradicated by Timur in the fourteenth century, and since then Christian influence has waxed and waned. During the time of the Soviet occupation, and even afterward, some Christian ministry was possible, but with the takeover of the Taliban, all Christian missionaries and most Westerners have been expelled. Expatriates are permitted to meet in small private home fellowships, but no evangelism is permitted and Afghanis may not visit. The few Afghani believers live in constant fear and suspicion of outsiders and potential new believers. Afghanistan's church has been in decline, primarily through death due to war and assassination, and losses due to emigration.

PERSECUTION

The Taliban has declared a new theocratic government based on a strict interpretation of shari'a law. Freedom of religion is severely restricted and is determined primarily by evolving, unwritten policies of the various factions. Most parts of the nation see a vigorous promotion of Islam, which has led to at least one martyr and, in general, to more oppression of the tiny Christian community than ever before. Custom and law require affiliation with some religion; atheism is considered apostasy, a crime punishable by death. All Afghanis are determined by default to be Muslims; conversion is illegal, and converts can be sentenced to death for apostasy. Non-Muslims in the country may practice their faith but not evangelize. All Muslim men must attend the daily prayers; Muslim women are not permitted to enter mosques and must pray at home. Afghanistan has been supported with imams (clerics), funds, and literature from other nations including Iran and Saudi Arabia. It is home to many radical Muslims who have often threatened Christians with death. The north of Afghanistan is a principle provider of the world's opium, and growers and dealers oppose Christians who take a stand against their trade.

Afghani believers, like Noor Khan, risk constant danger. One day Noor received a notice to appear at a government office. The reason given did not seem legitimate to him, but he prayed and went anyway. When he stepped into the building, officials grabbed him and demanded to know if he was Noor Khan, the man they suspected of being a Christian.

Afghanis often go by different names in different circumstances, so while some people knew him as Noor Khan, his legal name was totally different, so he told the officials they were mistaken and he presented his real name and papers.

They continued for hours to abuse Noor and accuse him of being a Christian. Finally they relented and locked him up, warning, "Just wait until the interrogators from Kandahar get here. They will get the truth out of you." Noor Khan could do nothing but wait and pray.

The next day three men arrived to question him. To his shock, he recognized one as his commander in the former Communist government's army. Noor Khan's heart sank as he realized the man would surely give him away. Instead, the visitor signaled to him to keep quiet and not let on that they knew each other. Later, when they were alone, the visitor explained, "If you don't tell them who I am, I won't tell them who you are and I will help you get out of here."

He was concerned for his own safety, because former Communists were routinely executed or imprisoned for their past crimes. This former Communist commander had been sent by Noor Khan's heavenly Commander and Lord to be Noor's deliverer.

THE FUTURE

The church in Afghanistan is presently in decline due to warfare and persecution. By 2050, without a major evangelistic thrust that would probably bear a significant price in martyrs, Afghanistan will continue to be solidly Muslim and restrictions will still be severe. It is unlikely that any secular trend will open the country to the gospel, since few Western nations have any significant business dealings with Afghanistan, and the principle trade and development partners are Islamic.

PRAYERS FOR THE SUFFERING

1. *The leaders of Afghanistan are intent upon making the nation one of the strictest Muslim countries on Earth.* Pray for the leaders of Afghanistan, particularly the Taliban, to come to know Jesus Christ as their personal Savior and to open the nation to Christian workers.

2. *Christian ministries have been expelled.* It is unlikely that they will be officially invited to return in the near future. Pray for Christian ministries to find innovative ways to enter Afghanistan and serve its people.

3. *Many Afghani refugees live abroad.* Often these are the more liberal Afghani intellectuals who disagree with the severity of the regime and could be open to Christianity. Some of these, if converted, may be called of the Lord to return to their homeland to bring the gospel to their families.

4. *Afghani believers keep their faith a deep secret in order to avoid persecution and death.* Pray for them to be given boldness and wisdom in order to survive and minister in this extremely hostile environment.

5. *Afghani women have been dramatically affected by the new regime.* The strict interpretation of Muslim law has denied them access to education, commerce, and medical care. They are severely isolated, particularly from the gospel. Pray for the discovery of creative avenues of ministry to them.

6. *Children have been terrible victims of the constant wars.* Many were wounded or killed by antipersonnel land mines deployed by the Soviets to suppress the *mujahaddin* freedom fighters. Pray that relief ministries will find ways to minister the love of Christ to them.

Please Pray for the Persecuted Church in:

ALGERIA

POPULATION 31.4 million (56% urban)	**CHRISTIANS** 90,000, share declining
LAND Northern Africa; 919,595 sq. miles (2,381,741 sq. km)	**PERSECUTION** Harassment, growing
LANGUAGES Arabic, Berber dialects, French	**RESTRICTIONS & FREEDOMS** Muslims may not convert Converts may be arrested, imprisoned, ostracized
RELIGION 99% Muslim	**IN THE 21ST CENTURY...** Islam will continue to present a formidable barrier to Christianity.

Algeria ranks among the largest nations on Earth, second largest in Africa, and eleventh in the world. The Sahara Desert takes up over nine-tenths of Algeria's territory; plains along the ocean are separated from the sands by mountains. Located in western North Africa, its neighbors include Tunisia and Libya to the east, Morocco to the west, and Mali, Mauritania, and Niger to the south.

Of the more than thirty million residents, some 90 percent are located in the coastal Tell region. As with most countries in North Africa and the Middle East, Algeria has a very youthful population: 40 percent are under fifteen and 30 percent are between fifteen and twenty-nine. Algeria's rapid growth means it will double its population in just thirty years. Eighty percent of Algeria's populace is Arabic, while the remaining 20 percent belong to one of the many Berber tribes. A little more than half live in the cities; Algiers, the capital, is the largest city with two million residents.

Villages found in archaeological digs have been dated back to 200,000 B.C. Carthage was an important civic and cultural center but it fell with the rest of the area to the Roman Empire in 146 B.C. Romans maintained control until the fifth century, after which the Vandals and then the Byzantines held power. It was during this latter period that Christianity was introduced. In the seventh century, Islam got its foothold and spread its influence all over North Africa. Several Muslim empires rose and fell, century after century. During this time,

YFOR US / ALGERIA

nary population became mobile with the increase of Bedouin immigrants. Ottomans established control in 1536.

Today Algeria is a multiparty republic. The government is presently battling
an intense insurgency, sparked by Muslim militants in 1992 after government
authorities canceled a general election that the now banned fundamentalist Islamic
Salvation Front was poised to win. More than 75,000 have died in the subsequent years of violence. The government censors all postal mail and controls
the media. Algeria faces severe economic problems, with an estimated 40 percent unemployment rate.

Most Algerians are Muslims. The government has attempted to keep Algeria
a moderate Islamic nation, while the fundamentalists desire the complete
establishment of an Islamic state.

CHURCH LIFE

Christianity came to Algeria in the first centuries after Christ, and some of the early
church's most prominent theologians (Ter-
tullian, Cyprian, Augustine) came from
Algeria. The church was weakened by disputes, Berber uprisings, and Vandal attacks
in the mid-400s. It was much reduced by
invading Muslim armies in A.D. 700 but rapidly
increased with the arrival of French settlers
in the early part the 1800s. With their withdrawal, the church again declined dramati-
cally. Nearly a third of the believers in Algeria are expatriates. Although there
are thousands of Algerian believers, they represent less than one half percent
of the total Algerian population, and they worship only in secret house churches.

PERSECUTION

Sunni Islam is Algeria's state religion, and Christian witness is not allowed.
Christian workers are often attacked and harassed by extremists, and many workers in Algeria have been martyred. Perhaps the most publicized case in recent
history was that of the seven Trappist monks who had lived and ministered in
Algeria since World War II and were abducted and murdered by Muslim fundamentalists. An Algerian believer writes:

"Everyone knows about the terrorism that has held our country in an iron grip. There have been few casualties among the evangelical Christians, for which we praise God. It is difficult to estimate the number of evangelical believers here but we think it lies between six and twelve thousand. A large majority comes from Berber background and only a few from Arab descent. Many of these live in small towns and villages, which makes it difficult to reach them.

"Because of the terrorism, travel within the country is very difficult, which means churches become isolated. We have few visitors from the West, and we cannot get permission to travel abroad either.

"Christian literature in Berber and Arabic is not readily available and cannot be freely distributed. In spite of all our difficulties, the church continues to grow."

THE FUTURE

It is likely that in the near future Algeria will manage some sort of peaceful settlement with the insurgents. Even if this does not stop all of the fighting, a certain amount of it will likely cease. Whether this will give Christians any measure of freedom to evangelize is doubtful. It is far more likely that Christians in Algeria will remain a persecuted minority, at least for the next few decades, until the common perception of Christianity as a "foreign religion" is somehow lessened.

PRAYERS FOR THE SUFFERING

1. *The church suffers from its image as a foreign religion.* Pray that it will develop a distinctly Algerian nature and culture.

2. *Many Catholic monasteries have earned the respect of Algerians for their unstinting aid to all.* Pray that respect for the church as a whole will continue to grow.

3. *Believers suffer from the ongoing, intense unrest and are special targets of radicals.* Pray for those Christians who have suffered attacks and for the many who have been left behind when loved ones have been martyred.

4. *Believers are helped in small ways by the government's stance against radicals.* Pray that the government will continue to maintain a moderate state and permit growing freedoms for Christians to worship. Pray that the

government will effect a peace agreement of some kind with the opposition in order to reduce the current tensions.

5. *Christians and all Algerians have been hurt by the ongoing war.* Much of the nation's infrastructure and its ability to provide for its people have been damaged. Pray for new opportunities for Christian relief ministries to work in Algeria.

Please Pray for the Persecuted Church in:

AZERBAIJAN

POPULATION	**CHRISTIANS**
7.7 million (56% urban)	350,000, share declining
LAND	**PERSECUTION**
Southwestern Asia, land-locked; 33,436 sq. miles (86,600 sq. km)	Harassment, static
	RESTRICTIONS & FREEDOMS
	Freedom of religion
LANGUAGES	
Azerbaijani, Russian, Armenian	**IN THE 21ST CENTURY...**
	Church growth is a perceived threat to Muslims; a widespread revival of Islam has been linked to growing nationalism and will provide a context for opposing Christianity.
RELIGION	
80% Muslim, 17% non-religious	

Azerbaijan is a small country located between Russia and Iran on the Caspian Sea. The large majority are Azerbaijani, but there are some small minority groups (including the Kurds and Lezgin) as well as many foreign expatriates working in the land. Russians and Armenians have both been rapidly leaving the country due to the internal conflicts in the area. About one-third of Azerbaijanis are under the age of fifteen; the population is growing slowly and is not expected to double before 2050. The nation is split fairly evenly between rural and urban dwellers; Baku, the capital and largest city, has 2.5 million residents; other cities number only a few hundred thousand.

Oil is the principle industry, and Azerbaijan has enormous deposits. There is vast economic potential for the country if it can exploit these resources; it is attempting to do so with Western help. Azerbaijan has switched to a market economy, but there is much urban poverty.

Azerbaijan has long been occupied by surrounding empires, the latest being the Soviet Union, from which it gained independence in 1991. Nationalists took control of the government in 1992, and the government has had warm relations with Turkey. Open war has been waged with Armenia for some time.

Although officially there is religious freedom, Muslims are the dominant force in the government and, following the war with Armenia, have become more

23

and more anti-Christian. A large minority of the population is nonreligious, following the deep impact of the Soviet Union.

CHURCH LIFE

There are perhaps 350,000 Christians in the country, the vast majority of whom are Orthodox believers. Less than a thousand are Protestants, mostly Baptists. These numbers are in a state of constant change since nearly all of the believers are foreign expatriates, mostly Russians and Armenians. Azerbaijani converts number less than a hundred.

PERSECUTION

Islamic revival has caused many Azerbaijanis to be less open to Christianity.

Few countries have experienced deterioration of freedom of religion as Azerbaijan did in 1996 and 1997. The government has almost started a war against converts, both by using direct pressure—interrogations, harassment, forcing Christians out of jobs, limitations in the distribution of Christian materials—and indirectly, by stirring up the man in the street against converts, resulting in shootings at a pastor, and children of Christians being harassed in schools.

Azerbaijani Baptists who had been operating a Christian street library in the western town of Gyanja were recently threatened by police twice "to halt preaching the gospel among Muslims," according to Baptist Pastor Ivan Orlov in the Azerbaijani capital of Baku. In January 2000, two of the Baptist men were detained. "They had just put out the religious literature on the library table when several police officers and an Azeri in civilian clothes led them off to the police station, taking the literature with them," Pastor Orlov said. "There they insulted and threatened them."

The Baptists belong to a congregation of the Council of Churches of Evangelical Christians/Baptists, an independent group that refused to register during the Soviet period. The denomination has retained this stand in all the post-Soviet republics where it operates.

Protestant Christians have suffered a number of difficulties operating in Azerbaijan, where the majority of the Azeri population is of Muslim background. Some Muslims and government officials have expressed strong disapproval that Christians are allowed to function. The closing months of 1999 were particularly difficult. As a result, President Haidar Aliev issued a public pledge in early November to enforce Azerbaijan's constitutional guarantees of freedom of conscience.

Within two weeks of Aliev's publicized pledge, the Supreme Court of Azerbaijan overturned deportation orders against eight expatriates arrested during a police raid of the Baku Baptist Church in September.

Disputes over permission for foreign clerics to serve local Christian congregations also appeared to be resolved. Visas were granted to two overseas clerics to continue to pastor the churches.

Despite the above intermittent difficulties, the Baptists say they intend to continue their evangelistic work. "We ask you to pray for us that the Lord will inspire us fearlessly to preach the good news about Christ at all times."

THE FUTURE

The presence of the church in Azerbaijan is, for the moment, largely dependent on the presence of foreign Christians, many of whom are more inclined to leave the country due to the internal conflicts. The indigenous Azerbaijani church is miniscule and, without outside assistance, is unable to reach the nation. For the near future it is unlikely that Christianity will grow to any sizable share of the population.

PRAYERS FOR THE SUFFERING

1. *Believers have suffered as a result of the Muslim-Christian nature of the Azerbaijan-Armenia conflict.* Pray for an improvement in relations between Christians and Muslims and a softening of tensions caused by the Azerbaijan-Armenia war.

2. *Missionaries are not overly welcomed in Azerbaijan.* Pray for foreign expatriates to find ways to serve Azerbaijan and to reach out in loving ministry to Azerbaijanis.

3. *The church has enjoyed some freedom.* Pray that growing resistance to Christianity will be divinely reduced and that the church will use its freedom to evangelize.

4. *The church has suffered from poverty.* Pray for Christian businesspeople to assist Azerbaijani Christians with new enterprise programs designed to alleviate the terrible blight of poverty in the cities.

Please Pray for the Persecuted Church in:

BAHRAIN

POPULATION	PERSECUTION
617,000 (91% urban)	Isolated, declining

LAND	RESTRICTIONS & FREEDOMS
Southwestern Asian islands (in Persian Gulf); 267 sq. miles (691 sq. km)	Freedom to worship Evangelism is illegal but possible

LANGUAGES	IN THE 21ST CENTURY...
Arabic, English, Farsi, Urdu	Although ministry is restricted, there will be little personal danger, and Christians will continue to be favorably welcomed and well thought of in a general sense.

RELIGION	
85% Muslim, 6% Hindu, 7% Christian	

CHRISTIANS	
43,000, share growing	

Bahrain is a group of several small islands in the Persian Gulf near Qatar and Saudi Arabia. The population is mainly Arab, with large minorities of Iranian, Indian, Pakistani, and European expatriate workers. With few exceptions, all live in the cities, of which the largest numbers some 150,000.

Although the economy is still largely centered on oil (which makes up more than 60 percent of exported products), Bahrain has diversified to become an important center of banking and industry. More than half the work force is expatriate, with workers arriving in Bahrain from nearly fifty countries.

Bahrain was taken by the Portuguese as a colony in 1550. In 1820 it became a British protectorate, and it was granted independence in 1971. In 1973 Bahrain was declared a constitutional monarchy, but it changed to an absolute monarchy in 1975. The nation is ruled by the Emir; a forty-member consultative council serves simply as an advisory body. No political parties are permitted.

Bahrain provides comprehensive public health care for all its citizens. Most of the children are enrolled in primary school, and a large majority of the population is literate.

Islam is the official religion of the state and the religion of virtually all Bahraini citizens. Although a sizable minority practice the Sunni tradition, most follow the Shi'a tradition. These are split between urban Sunnis and rural and Iranian Shi'ites.

CHURCH LIFE

A Christian bishopric was established in Bahrain in the third century after Christ. Protestant missions began in the area in the early 1900s. Bahrain has been a good base for Christian witness throughout the last century, and there remain many opportunities for tactful sharing of faith. Despite restrictions on evangelism, Christian expatriate churches are permitted and even welcomed. There are dozens of churches, but nearly all of the Christians are expatriates.

PERSECUTION

Islam is the official religion of the country, and there is a strong bias against Christianity. Expatriate Christians are granted freedom of worship but no evangelism of Muslims is permitted. At the same time Christians, and some of their

ministries, are highly regarded and well thought of, particularly the American Mission Hospital. There is also a Christian bookstore that sells Christian literature to the public.

THE FUTURE

Despite the tactful outpouring of Christian witness there are few Bahraini believers, and the indigenous church is not growing at a rapid pace. It is unlikely that, outside of the expatriate witness, Christianity will claim a sizable number of adherents in Bahrain until late in this century, if then.

PRAYERS FOR THE SUFFERING

1. *The church enjoys freedom of worship.* Pray that Muslims will be drawn to Christian worship services and be able to discreetly visit.

2. *Christian bookstores are permitted to operate.* Pray that they will be permitted to continue to sell Christian literature and that Muslims will frequent the stores.

3. *The church suffers from a social bias against Christianity.* Pray that Christians will find new ways to soften the prejudices and earn the favor of the government and the general populace.

4. *The church has been able to serve the nation through the American Mission Hospital.* Praise God for the substantial medical ministry and pray that it may be broadened.

5. *The church suffers from a lack of global interest.* Pray that the global body of Christ will expand the provision of evangelistic resources to the Bahraini church.

Please Pray for the Persecuted Church in:

BANGLADESH

POPULATION	**PERSECUTION**
126.1 million (19% urban)	Isolated, growing
LAND	**RESTRICTIONS & FREEDOMS**
Southern Asia; 55,598 sq. miles (143,998 sq. km)	Limited freedom to evangelize
LANGUAGES	Potential blasphemy law
Bangla, English	**IN THE 21ST CENTURY...**
RELIGION	The greatest struggle the church will face is to adequately minister in the midst of enormous poverty.
85% Muslim	
CHRISTIANS	
580,000, share growing	

Bangladesh occupies the floodplains of the Ganges and Brahmaputra Rivers east of India, and as a result, receives major quantities of rain and is subjected to frequent floods.

More than 126 million people live in Bangladesh, making it the sixth most populous nation in the world. The people of Bangladesh are mostly rural; less than 20 percent live in cities. Nearly two-thirds are under the age of fifteen, making Bangladesh a very young country; nevertheless, the population is growing slowly and isn't expected to double until late this century. Bengalis make up 95 percent of the population, but they have been divided by religion between Muslim and Hindu Bengalis. About 3 percent of the population is made up of minority groups, both tribals and expatriates.

Bangladesh is one of the world's poorest nations; it suffers from overpopulation and frequent natural disasters such as devastating floods and cyclones with enormous loss of life. These, coupled with corruption, have stood in the way of any concerted effort at uplifting the living standard of the people. In the near future there seems little hope that poverty will be substantially alleviated. Over half of the work force is unemployed.

Jute, one of its main exports, has fallen on hard times with the rise in popularity of plastic. There is a small, privileged group of rich people and a very large group of the poor. Because of a lack of jobs at home, many Bangladeshis have gone in search of work in the Middle East, Singapore, and Malaysia.

Until 1947 the country was known as East Bengal in India. In 1947, when Pakistan became an independent nation, this block of predominantly Muslim land became known as East Pakistan. Then in 1971 a bitter civil war of independence was fought, ending in the defeat of the resident Pakistani administration by Bangladeshi forces aided by India. Corruption, instability, assassinations, and eighteen coups have marred the years since then. A nine-year military dictatorship ended in 1991 with restoration of democracy and the election of a government led by Begum Khaleda Zia, a woman.

From 1971–88 Bangladesh was a secular state; then the government declared Islam to be the state religion. This has heightened tension between Muslims and followers of other religions. The political turmoil that plagued the country in recent years appears to have ended with the June 1996 elections, but some political tension will likely continue. The nation is now concentrating on rebuilding.

Muslims make up about 85 percent of the population, most of whom adhere to the Sunni branch of Islam. Hindus comprise most of the remainder, but there are small numbers of Buddhists, animists, and Christians. Hindus suffered severe losses due to deaths and refugee movements in the 1971 civil war, but despite their smaller numbers they remain a vocal and influential minority to this day.

CHURCH LIFE

Catholic missionaries were among the first Christians to enter Bangladesh, arriving in the sixteenth century. Bangladesh was deeply impacted by the ministry of Protestant missionary William Carey, who opened work in the land in 1795. Nonetheless, despite the extensive ministry of Christian missionaries throughout the decades, Christians number only a small part of the nation today.

Nearly all converts from Islam are secret believers, although there are a few instances of whole villages turning to Christ and worshiping publicly. Most public Christians, however, are converts from low-caste Hindu peasants and small tribes (the latter of which have proven to be the most receptive to Christianity). The small overall number of Christians (about 580,000) and the denominational division

31

(at least 32 denominations) among them both weaken their position enormously. Catholics have the largest share: some 250,000 members. Protestants number about the same but are divided by denominations. Neither tradition is heavily involved in evangelism; Christian ministries over the years have been heavily concentrated in the realm of education.

PERSECUTION

While the government has prudently chosen not to jeopardize Western aid by openly espousing Islamization, it has become clear in recent years that Bangladesh policy will increasingly take on a more Islamic stance. One prominent church leader predicted recently that missionaries would no longer be granted visas. In fact, he did not think missionaries would be allowed to remain in Bangladesh.

Although Muslim fundamentalists are a small minority, they are relentless in their effort to exert pressure on the current government to bring Bangladesh under shari'a rule. With increasing participation of Islamic countries, particularly from the Middle East, in the aid program of the nation, the government finds that it has to make concessions to Muslim sentiments. This could drastically affect the rights of non-Muslim citizens.

One such issue is the Islamic fundamentalist party Jamaat-i-Islami's call to introduce the blasphemy law, similar to the one currently in force in Pakistan. Both non-Muslims and many liberal, intellectual Muslims have voiced their opposition to it. Fortunately, the Islamization policy introduced by the former government may have taken a backseat in the face of stark economic realities that the present government has committed itself to tackle. With the more secular Jatiya Party of former President Ershad as its political coalition partner, we may see the waning of Jamaat-i-Islami's influence.

Since Cushi and his wife gave their lives in faith to the Lord Jesus, they have faced strong opposition from their staunchly Muslim relatives and community. First, their house was set on fire when they refused to recant their faith in Jesus before their Muslim relatives. Then no shop owner would allow them to buy or eat in their store. Even Cushi's meager crop—his family's only source of livelihood (after he lost his job also on account of his faith) was confiscated. But the hardest and most painful of all was to see Shila, his eleven-year-old daughter, endure hardship in school because her parents had turned away from Islam.

More than once Cushi has been threatened with death, but he has remained strong in the faith. His is not a reckless kind of courage but comes from a calm assurance that God has the power and ability to deliver him and his family from death. He says, "I am not afraid to die. I will work for God; I will talk to the people about God."

And God blesses him for his faithfulness. Soon people started coming to him despite stern warnings from the Islamic leaders. "It is not my word that they believe in, but God who is talking through me. They believe in God."

He is always on his feet, usually walking five or six miles' distance to the villages, wherever people are willing to hear his message. He had already won sixty people to the Lord before attending an Open Doors training seminar for lay preachers. Cushi has baptized fifteen more families, including some relatives and former persecutors.

His converts, like him, face myriad hardships. They are totally removed from society. They are not even allowed to use the community well from which they drew water. Their children are often barred from school and ostracized by their Muslim classmates. But the more opposition they experience, the more people come to the Lord.

Cushi is determined to continue the work of evangelization among his people and only requests prayer that God prepares their minds and hearts to hear and receive His Word.

THE FUTURE

There seems little hope that the poverty of this unhappy land, compounded by natural disasters, will ever be substantially alleviated. However, the church is increasing and will likely number more than two million by 2050. Even then, it will only form slightly more than 1 percent of the nation, having little influence or impact.

PRAYERS FOR THE SUFFERING

1. *The church suffers in the midst of extreme poverty.* Pray that Christians from around the world will be able to serve the needs of Bangladesh, particularly in the economic arena.

2. *Bangladesh has been wounded by numerous natural disasters.* Pray that the church will be able to develop systems for quickly responding to these nearly annual events.

3. *Observers are wary of the potential for a blasphemy law.* Pray that this law will be restrained and that the church will instead be afforded new freedoms.

4. *The nation has been hurt by political turmoil.* Pray that Christians will be ministers of healing, reconciliation, and a spirit of charity throughout the land.

Please Pray for the Persecuted Church in:

BHUTAN

POPULATION 2.1 million (6% urban), U.N. figures used	**PERSECUTION** Harassment, growing
LAND Southern Asia, landlocked; 17,954 sq. miles (46,500 sq. km)	**RESTRICTIONS & FREEDOMS** No evangelism No conversion
LANGUAGES Dzongkha, Tibetan, and Nepalese dialects	**IN THE 21ST CENTURY...** Buddhism will continue to form significant social and official barriers to Christianity, and converts will face serious consequences for their decision.
RELIGION 70% Buddhist, 25% Hindu	
CHRISTIANS 9,000, declining	

K nown as *Druk Yul*, or *"The Land of the Thunder Dragon,"* the tiny kingdom of Bhutan is nestled high in the Himalayan Mountains. It is essentially built on a slope descending 20,000 feet from the northern range of high, snow-capped mountains separating it from Tibet, one of the five autonomous regions of China. The population here is sparse and the slopes are covered with birch, magnolia, and rhododendron, while for many months of the year the summits are decked with snow.

Bhutan was settled by a series of migrations through the centuries from the surrounding areas, but principally from Tibet. Its population of just over two million is divided among four major cultures (Tibetan, Indian, Southeast Asian, Nepali). Rugged mountainous terrain and extremes of climate have made the Bhutanese a hardy, well-built people, accustomed to hard work. Despite the strong, martial spirit that has enabled them to retain their national independence and sovereignty over the years, they are peaceful and fun-loving.

Cloistered in its mountain sanctuary forbidden to all foreigners until 1974, Bhutan has marched to the beat of its own drummer for centuries. The country is still not enthused about the idea of strangers trekking through its winding valleys and its only recently paved streets. In 1990, ostensibly to protect Bhutanese culture from outside influences, King Jigme Singyhe Wangchuk ordered further measures to maintain its isolation.

Central Bhutan is the economic and cultural heartland of the country. The nation has been noted as environmentally one of the richest countries in the world; however, this is not reflected in the economy. The government's policy is one of sustainable development while ensuring the preservation of natural resources. Nearly all are involved in subsistence farming and animal husbandry; rice is the principal crop. The society is arranged in three groups—nobility, peasantry, and slaves (although the latter have been officially freed). Less than 20 percent of the adults are literate.

Bhutan's spiritual umbilical cord is tied both historically and theologically to neighboring Tibet. Mahayana Buddhism is practiced by three-quarters of the population. Often referred to as Tibetan Buddhism, the religion repudiates God

and steeps itself in animism and the occult; demons have become as familiar to this religion's practitioners as cliff-hugging monasteries, prayer flags, and prayer wheels. It was introduced in Bhutan in the eighth century. About one-quarter of the population (mostly Nepalis) are Hindus.

CHURCH LIFE

There is no official Christian church, although some 9,000 believers are estimated to live within Bhutan, most ethnic Nepali or Indian.

PERSECUTION

In the thirteenth century Phage Drogue Shiga made the Drukpa school of Kagyupa Buddhism preeminent in Bhutan, and this sect is still the state religion. Evangelism by any other religion, in any form, is illegal. The numerous monasteries, and thousands of monks, play an important role as centers of higher culture, keeping alive traditions; their combined influence on the society serves as a cultural barrier to the gospel. They are consulted as physicians, for the conduct of most social ceremonies such as weddings and funerals, and to cast horoscopes and perform the important religious rituals associated with every detail of daily life.

Aside from being socially ostracized, the church is often subject to government harassment. Church buildings may be torn down for no reason. Trumped-up charges are sometimes leveled at believers. Pastors and evangelists have been arrested, jailed, tortured, and killed.

THE FUTURE

The Christian church in Bhutan is small and its share of the population is presently in decline. Although it is adding to its numbers (mainly through births to Christian households) and may reach as many as 30,000 believers by 2050, its growth rate is only half that of the population as a whole.

PRAYERS FOR THE SUFFERING

1. *The church endures global interest in the preservation of Buddhist culture.* Bhutan receives substantial global aid and attention for its Buddhist community, and the result is the communication of overwhelming support for Buddhism in general. Pray for more support to be raised for the Christian church in Bhutan.

2. *Christians are subject to sporadic yet constant harassment.* Pray for pastors who find their churches burned, for congregations who find their pastors arrested, and for the widows and orphans of those martyred.

3. *Pastors and evangelists pay a tremendous price.* They work despite the threats, trusting God to protect and deliver them and their families. Water baptism is the point at which the greatest persecution occurs because of its very public nature. Pray for strength for the church to endure.

Please Pray for the Persecuted Church in:

BRUNEI

POPULATION	**PERSECUTION**
328,000 (70% urban)	Harassment, static
LAND	**RESTRICTIONS & FREEDOMS**
Southeastern Asia (island of Borneo); 2,226 sq. miles (5,765 sq. km)	Limited freedom of worship No evangelism
LANGUAGES	**IN THE 21ST CENTURY...**
Malay, English, Chinese, Tamil	The enormous influence of the government's subsidies will form significant social barriers to the gospel.
RELIGION	
75% Muslim	
CHRISTIANS	
25,000, static	

Brunei is a narrow coastal plain with a hilly interior, located on the northwest tip of the island of Borneo. Dense swamps and a humid, climate mark the area; rain forests cover much of the interior.

The country has about 328,000 inhabitants. Two-thirds of them are Malays, and 15 percent are Chinese. About a third of the people are under the age of fifteen. Approximately two-thirds of the population lives in urban areas and the rest are in rural villages.

In 1425 the Hindu ruler of Brunei, Awang Alak Betatar, was converted to Islam and invited Arab scholars to begin missionary work in the country. From the fifteenth to the seventeenth centuries Brunei Darussalam (full name) was the seat of a powerful sultanate extending over Sabah, Sarawak, and the lower Philippines. Thus, the current sultan represents one of the oldest continuously ruling dynasties in the world. By the nineteenth century, the Brunei Darussalam Empire had been whittled away by wars, piracy, and the colonial expansion of European powers.

In 1888 Brunei Darussalam officially became a British protectorate. In 1906 the Residential System was established in Brunei Darussalam. A British resident advised the sultan in all matters except Malay customs, traditions, and Islamic religion. The 1959 agreement established a written constitution that gave Brunei Darussalam internal self-government. In 1971 the agreement was amended and revised to assert full internal independence, except defense and external affairs. On January 1, 1984, Brunei Darussalam resumed full independence.

Today Brunei is governed by the sultan, who rules by decree. The political culture encourages quiet acquiescence with his rule; the people are amply rewarded with free health care, free education, free recreational centers, cheap loans, and the highest per capita incomes on earth. The ostentatious modern public buildings notwithstanding, most of the country remains undeveloped, unexploited, and untouched by the outside world. The economy is completely dependent upon oil and gas.

Three-quarters of Brunei's people are Muslims. There are minorities of Buddhists, Hindus, and other Asian religions. The Islamic faith continues to make significant inroads among these minorities, seeing a steady annual stream of converts.

CHURCH LIFE

Christians number nearly 25,000 in twenty congregations, about 7 percent of the population. Anglicanism and Catholicism are the two largest traditions. Most of the believers are Chinese or Indians; there are very few Brunei believers. Most are expatriates working for the oil companies. The church has an active program of ministry through meetings, camps, and literature despite restrictions.

PERSECUTION

According to the constitution, Islam is the state religion and the sultan is the head of the faith. The free practice of other religions is guaranteed but in practice all evangelism is prohibited. Decrees in the early 1990s banned the importation of Christian literature and the public celebration of Christmas and forbade all public contacts with Christians in other countries. At the same time most of the Catholic priests and nuns were expelled. No Christians have publicly confessed their faith; secret believers remain safely anonymous. A brother from Brunei writes: "We are allowed to be Christians as long as we stay within limits. We can evangelize our own tribe, but definitely not the Muslims. In 1993 some Korean tourists tried public evangelism and sang on the streets. They were jailed for one night.

"Since 1992, control on Christian activities has intensified. When Christians from a neighboring country tried mailing in some Christian literature, the recipients were interrogated by the police and the books were confiscated.

"An indigenous denomination sought to construct buildings to house two new congregations but the government won't give permission to build any more churches. The two congregations have to continue meeting in private homes. In another instance, a church wanted to expand its present premises, but the authorities came and tore down the new wing. The church was told to stay within its original area. So the church resolved to vertical expansion—building more stories on the original site.

"Restrictions on Christianity are likely to intensify. The government knows that Christians are [numerically] on the increase and is trying to stop the trend. The government is also carrying out an Islamization effort, which has had some measure of success in converting young people to Islam. When one applies for certain jobs, one must first become a Muslim. In the workplace, Muslims also try to convert non-Muslim and Christian colleagues.

"What can we do in our situation? We can pray. About two years ago the Lord revealed to a brother of an intercessory group the location of a cave. The brother led a small expedition and followed the leading of the Lord for some distance outside the city. Then up a small hill they found a hole. They were disappointed at its size, but the Lord told them there was a bigger hole inside. With some explosives they broke through the first small hole and indeed found a sizable cave within. Since then about twenty Christians regularly go to the cave to fast and pray overnight. There we can cry out loudly to the Lord without other people hearing. It is much freer than other places.

"From the prayer cave, we pray for the salvation of more people. There have been prophecies about Brunei coming to Christ. We believe one day it will. We pray for the government, especially the ruler, believing God will do a miracle in his heart. We ask Christians outside of Brunei to stand with us in prayer. Pray that we will grow strong in faith although there is persecution. Pray that God will work greatly among us. Our country's full name is Negara (nation) Brunei Darussalam. The last word, *Darussalam*, means *abode of peace*—a variation of shalom. We hope our country will indeed be the abode of God's shalom one day."

THE FUTURE

Despite restrictions the church continues to grow at a moderate pace. At the current rate it will likely come close to doubling in size by 2050; unfortunately, the population will have doubled in the same period, so Christianity's share of the population will not likely have grown. Under this scenario it is doubtful much will have changed in the government's attitude toward the church.

PRAYERS FOR THE SUFFERING

1. *The church suffers from bans on its activity.* Pray that the government will uphold its guarantee of freedom of religion and lift the bans on Christian evangelism and worship. Pray that the government will soften its stance and permit Christian holidays to be celebrated by expatriates within the country.

2. *Official missionaries are not permitted in Brunei.* Pray that expatriate Christians will find quiet opportunities to share the gospel with the people of Brunei and that the number of Brunei believers will increase.

3. *The people are satiated with government-provided subsidies.* Pray that in its materialistic opulence the people of Brunei will become aware of their spiritual emptiness and need for Jesus Christ. Pray that there will be an increasing spiritual yearning that will lead them to seek out Christians.

Please Pray for the Persecuted Church in:

CAMBODIA

POPULATION 11.1 million (21% urban)	**PERSECUTION** Isolated, static
LAND Southeastern Asia; 69,898 sq. miles (181,035 sq. km)	**RESTRICTIONS & FREEDOMS** Freedom to worship Freedom to evangelize
LANGUAGES Khmer, French	**IN THE 21ST CENTURY...** The church will have a slowly increasing influence on the country.
RELIGION 95% Buddhist; 4% folk-religionists	
CHRISTIANS Less than 100,000 but share rapidly growing	

Cambodia is located in Southeastern Asia, bordering the Gulf of Thailand, between Thailand, Vietnam, and Laos. It is marked by low, flat plains in the center, bounded by mountains in the southwest and the north. More than two-thirds of Cambodia is covered with forested woodlands.

More than eleven million people live in Cambodia. Nearly half are under the age of fifteen. A bit more than 20 percent live in urban areas, while the large majority live in small, rural villages. The Khmer make up about 85.2 percent of the population, but there are several small minority groups, including the Cham, the Mnong, and the Paong. Additionally, there are Vietnamese, Chinese, and Lao immigrants. The capital, Phnom Penh, has over one million residents.

Cambodia is a multiparty liberal democracy under a constitutional monarchy established in September 1993. Cambodia was affected by the Vietnam conflict in the 1970s and has experienced ongoing conflict ever since. There is political freedom but much hardship still remains.

Cambodia was a powerful kingdom between the first and fourteenth centuries. With its decline, it became a pawn in regional and global conflicts with the Thai, Vietnamese, French, Japanese, and Americans. Cambodia was a tragic victim of the Vietnam War, which opened the way to the extreme Marxist Khmer Rouge takeover in 1975, followed by one of the most savage slaughters in the twentieth century. Almost all the wealthy, educated, and political families were killed, and the rest turned into a vast labor camp. The Vietnamese ousted the Khmer Rouge in 1978, but the civil war between four contending armies raged with superpower support until 1991.

Cambodians earn less than U.S.$1,000 annually, although the economy is growing. Nearly everyone works in occupations related to agriculture. Years of devastation caused serious financial problems in the nation, and though their situation is improving, many problems remain: little more than half of adults are literate, much of the country's infrastructure has been destroyed, and they have little access to technology.

Nearly 90 percent of the population practices Buddhism. Some 3 percent are Muslim, and another 3 percent practice traditional animistic faiths.

CHURCH LIFE

Only about 1 percent of Cambodians are Christians. However, with the overthrow of the Khmer Rouge, increasing freedoms have come to the land in the 1990s, bringing with them the freedom to evangelize. Christians are generally looked upon as second-class citizens, but they have begun to have a wider impact through the sharing of the gospel. Evangelistic programs have been aired on television and Christian musical concerts have been held in the capital.

PERSECUTION

During the rule of the Khmer Rouge, Christians and Buddhist monks were slaughtered ruthlessly. With the new government persecution has significantly lessened. While there is some harassment of the church, there is complete freedom to worship and evangelize.

THE FUTURE

Christians number nearly 100,000, and their share of the country's population is rapidly growing. By 2050 they could well number nearly a million adherents, most of whom will be members of indigenous Cambodian churches.

PRAYERS FOR THE SUFFERING

1. *The church is enjoying an enormous wave of freedom.* Praise God for this open opportunity to evangelize Cambodia, and pray that it is used to the greatest effect by the church.

2. *Many converts are insincere, converting for economic benefits.* A large number backslide under pressure from Buddhists. Pray that the church will be able to reap and retain converts and equip them adequately for evangelism.

3. *Persecution continues sporadically.* Pray for the seekers and pastors who must contend with harassment from radicals and the government.

Please Pray for the Persecuted Church in:

CHAD

POPULATION	**PERSECUTION**
7.6 million (23% urban)	Isolated, declining
LAND	**RESTRICTIONS & FREEDOMS**
Central Africa, landlocked; 495,755 sq. miles (1,284,000 sq. km)	Freedom to worship Freedom to evangelize
LANGUAGES	**IN THE 21ST CENTURY...**
Arabic, French, indigenous	The country faces the danger of becoming yet
RELIGION	another Sudan, but the church has a limited
60% Muslim; 17% tribal	window of opportunity to make a significant impact
CHRISTIANS	on the nation.
1.5 million, share increasing	

The northern third of Chad is made up of deserts, with mountains in the far north. In the center lies a broad, arid savanna, with Lake Chad in the west and highlands in the east. Wooded, humid lowlands with numerous rivers mark the southern third.

The presence of Lake Chad has been a magnet drawing many cultures and peoples into the region, contributing to the enormous ethnic mix in the land. Some 7.5 million reside in Chad, most of them concentrated around the capital city and the southern third of the nation. French and Arabic are the official languages, although Sara is common in the south, and more than one hundred languages are used by the two hundred distinct ethnic groups. In the north, Toubou form the majority group, while Arabs are found frequently in the center and the Sara in the south.

Chad was once a French colony, and during French rule the south gained primary importance. With independence in 1960, northerners came to resent southern dominance in the new government. Factionalism sparked by ethnic and religious disagreements helped incite open warfare, which has taken on a decidedly religious aspect, pitting the Muslim north against the Christian-animist south in a war reminiscent of Sudan.

This war, along with drought, famine, and declining prices for cotton, have made Chad one of Africa's poorest nations. It has an estimated gross national product of U.S.$160 per capita. Chad's primary export is cotton, which is grown in the south. About 15 percent of adults are literate, and less than half of all children attend school. Health care is virtually nonexistent, and life is short, averaging about forty years.

More than half of the population is Muslim. The rest adhere to traditional African religions or Christianity.

CHURCH LIFE

Early Christian missionary efforts led to the successful planting of several denominations in the southern third of Chad. Today this remains the strongest base of Christianity in the country. Chad's 1.5 million believers add nearly 40,000 new members annually, most through births to Christian homes.

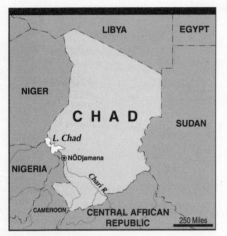

PERSECUTION

The country has been dominated by internal strife between the Muslim north and the Christian and animist south. Christians were heavily persecuted in the 1970s under the rule of President Ngarta Tombalbaye, who was assassinated in a coup in 1975. There has been relative freedom of religion under a secular state since. Even so, it doesn't stop individuals pushed by religious zeal from doing what they want to do.

Early Christmas morning, 1999, Christians in Mangalmé, which is near Mongo in the southern third of Chad, awoke to a bitter sight. Someone had set fire to their chapel just hours after they had held Christmas Eve prayers there.

Distinct shoe prints were found at the scene, and police arrested a man and two others soon after. Tensions had been running high between Christians and Muslims, but the local Islamic council denied any involvement and even stated that the main perpetrator was not Muslim. Determined to overcome the setback, church members rebuilt the chapel, only to have it burned down again. This time the local Islamic council offered to help rebuild the chapel and even post its own guard there. At first the church rejected the offer. The second burning was a great discouragement. Moreover, many Christians who were working in the civil service or para-civil service considered leaving Mangalmé because it had become too dangerous. According to a church member, the prefect from nearby Mongo investigated the second fire and found the real culprit: a fundamental Islamic group that acts independently from the Islamic council of Mangalmé—a group "that is able to do worse evil than just burning the chapel." After much discussion, the Christians decided to stay in Mangalmé and rebuild the chapel once again, trusting God to keep them safe.

THE FUTURE

The expansion of the gospel continues to be hampered by the clash of cultures between the north and the south. Christians number 1.5 million and continue to grow in terms of number of adherents, increasing their share of the nation as a whole. By 2050 they could very well double in size to more than three million.

PRAYERS FOR THE SUFFERING

1. *The church enjoys a current window of freedom.* Praise God for the freedom to worship and evangelize, and pray that the church will use it wisely.

2. *The north remains under-evangelized.* Pray that the church will reach out with evangelism initiatives to the Muslim population, despite the significant risk.

3. *The church has suffered along with the rest of the nation in Chad's deep poverty.* Pray that Christians in Chad and around the world will be able to serve the country with new solutions for its economic hardships.

Please Pray for the Persecuted Church in:

CHIAPAS, MEXICO

POPULATION	**PERSECUTION**
3.5 million	Continued, static
LAND	**RESTRICTIONS & FREEDOMS**
Southern Mexican state, mountainous; 28,653 sq. miles (74,211 sq. km)	Limited freedom to evangelize Harassment by local leaders
RELIGION	
94% Christian Christians approx. 30–40% evangelical as compared with 3–8% for other parts of Mexico	**IN THE 21ST CENTURY...** The church must reach out in love to those around it with a determined effort to evangelize its persecutors.
CHRISTIANS	
Protestants number several thousand	

A rticle 24 of the Mexican Constitution guarantees "every person is free to profess the religious beliefs that pleases him/her." However, evangelical Christians face unrelenting persecution in the Mexican state of Chiapas, often with the complicity of elected authorities. They are victims of a corrupting mixture of religion and politics.

Spanish colonials imposed Catholic Christianity on Mexico in the sixteenth century, but the restless tribes in the southern highlands did not entirely submit. Indigenous mystics, claiming to act in obedience to supernatural visions, convinced fellow Indians to preserve ancient Mayan religious concepts, such as worship of the earth and sun and the practice of fertility rites. These traditional beliefs fused with Roman Catholic dogma to produce the traditionalist Catholicism predominant in the area today.

After long periods of warfare, a cautious peace settled into Chiapas. Mestizos (Mexicans of mixed European and Amerindian descent) were able to peacefully coexist with their indigenous neighbors. The Mexican government ruled at a distance, allowing *caciques* to maintain order; the caciques, in turn, helped maintain a comfortable political atmosphere. The arrangement, unfortunately, did not help the residents of the area. The government has invested little in the poor residents, and the quality of life in the region is the lowest in all of

Mexico. Illiteracy is high, and per capita income is well below the poverty line. In effect, the caciques have a political and economic stranglehold on the region. Caciques impose religious taxes during the festivals; those who cannot pay must borrow the money at exorbitant interest rates. Further, by controlling the judiciary, the caciques can harass Protestants with impunity.

CHURCH LIFE

Despite persecution, Christians have been able to spread the gospel, and relations between Christians and other local residents have improved. In December 1999 one thousand participated in a symbolic march called the "Pilgrimage for the Renewal of Our Hearts"; a month later, more than thirty-six hundred people were baptized in the surf off Puerto Madero.

PERSECUTION

Protestant Christianity was introduced into the area after World War II. Despite persecution, missionaries and local Christians were able to finish a translation of the New Testament and commission evangelists to conduct church planting programs. These Christians had developed a new way of life: they refused to buy candles or consume alcohol, thus breaking the economic hold of

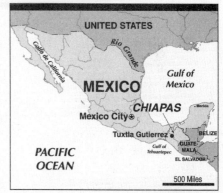

the caciques, who responded with violent attacks. Churches and homes have been destroyed by mobs; whole communities have been expelled from their homes; evangelistic outreaches have been harassed. Individual Christians have been assassinated, and some groups have been massacred.

Pascuala's story is an astonishing testimony of survival and victory. After becoming a Christian more than twenty years ago through the witness of a former witch doctor who had accepted Jesus as his Savior, she gave herself completely to the service of the Lord. "I experienced a change in my life; I felt that everything around me was new and I saw things in a different way. I stopped going to the *J'ilol* (witch doctor) because I learned that Jesus could heal our illnesses."

She used to tell everyone she could about the power and love of Jesus Christ, until her aunt Maria, one of the tribe witches, warned her "to be careful because the people are saying that they are going to burn down your house and kill you."

Pascuala recalls, "One night my nephew, three nieces, and I were in the house. We sang a hymn, prayed, and laid down to sleep peacefully. About midnight I was awakened by the barking of a dog, and I realized that the house was on fire. I grabbed a blanket and went outside to see what was happening. I saw someone aim a gun at me and shoot. I managed to scream at everyone to get out of the house. I ran in the dark, even crawled at times when I had no strength left in me. I got to a friend's house after a few hours, and I was given a coat and water to drink. Blood was flowing from my wounds. We set out walking, and at about 8:00 A.M. we arrived in San Cristobal de las Casas, where I was taken first to the Ministry of Public Affairs to file a legal report and then to the hospital."

Pascuala had twenty-one bullet wounds, but even worse, when the authorities checked her house they found that only one of her nieces had survived the attack. Despite the loss and the physical pain Pascuala still experiences from that night, she happily declares with the old hymn: "I have decided to follow Jesus . . . no turning back!"

THE FUTURE

The current leadership of the Catholic Church in Chiapas is in flux, at least in part for the role it plays in supporting religious freedom in the area. Future leaders may not be as helpful. Despite this, many evangelicals are optimistic about the future of religious freedom. The international community has grown in its awareness of Chiapas, and Mexico has begun to be pressured to enforce their rights.

PRAYERS FOR THE SUFFERING

1. *The church suffers because of poverty.* Many of the local believers are extremely poor. Pray that the body of Christ will be able to respond and help with programs and initiatives to lift them out of poverty.

2. *International pressure has been brought to bear.* Pray that this pressure will increase and that the government will continue to be responsive.

3. *Some Catholics have been sympathetic to the situation.* Pray that more of those in the leadership of the Roman Catholic Church will be open to religious freedom in the area.

4. *Some of the caciques have become peaceable.* Pray for the evangelization and conversion of these local "warlords" and that they will then be a strong witness to others.

Please Pray for the Persecuted Church in:

CHINA

The third largest country in the world, China is also the most populous and contains the highest mountains on the face of our planet. Most of China's population lives in the east, centered primarily in forty-two mega-cities with more than one million residents each.

China's residents speak more than six hundred dialects and are clustered in nearly two hundred ethnic groups (of which fifty-five are officially registered). About a quarter of the populace can't read, and although China has one of the world's fastest-growing economies, the average person is poor with an annual income of less than U.S.$500.

China's history extends back twenty-two centuries before Christ, and the Chinese people are extremely proud to belong to the oldest civilization in the world. The name *China* originated in the time of the Qin (or Ch'in) Dynasty (221–206 B.C.), when Qin Shi Huang was emperor. It means "Middle Kingdom"— ancient Chinese viewed themselves as being at the center of the world. A succession of dynasties ruled the nation until 1911, when Sun Yat-sen overthrew the Qing Dynasty. In the 1920s Chiang Kai-shek came to power, but the Communist Party, founded in 1921, fought with Chiang's Kuomintang (Nationalist Party) to control China. The factions temporarily cooperated against Japanese invasion but resumed conflict after World War II. Mao Zedong and the

POPULATION
1.25 billion (31% urban)

LAND
Eastern Asia; 3,690,045 sq. miles (9,557,172 sq. km)

LANGUAGES
Chinese dialects

RELIGION
Nonreligious 42%,
Folk religionists 28%,
Atheists 8%

CHRISTIANS
70 million, share growing

PERSECUTION
Sharp, sporadic change

RESTRICTIONS & FREEDOMS
No evangelism outside of registered churches
No evangelism of youth under 18
Churches must be registered
Pastors may be arrested, imprisoned, sentenced to labor camps

IN THE 21ST CENTURY…
Despite all persecution the church will continue to grow explosively; Chinese missionaries could even become the new power-house for global mission.

Communists achieved victory in 1949, and Chiang's Kuomintang Party retreated to Taiwan. Both parties' governments still officially claim sovereignty over all of China.

Although China officially has a Communist government, in reality it is governed by men, not laws. Those in power crave stability above everything else and labor to crush ruthlessly anything they perceive to be a threat. It is perhaps this fact that explains why the church is persecuted mercilessly in some areas while it has grown rapidly, and with little restraint, in others. The Communist Party has changed significantly from the days of Mao; under the late leader, Deng Xiaopeng, China opened its doors again to the rest of the world, and foreign trade with the West has been encouraged. Today Communist ideologies remain firmly in place but, economically, capitalism is the order of the day.

Some 60 percent of Chinese are nonreligious. Chinese religions and Buddhism make up another third, while Christians are estimated at between 6 and 10 percent, or some seventy million people. China's church is one of the fastest growing in the world. In theory, Christians are afforded personal freedom of religion, but their leeway to evangelize is limited. Children under the age of eighteen may not be evangelized; all churches must be registered; Christians may not meet in unregistered centers of worship; and Christians are not allowed to evangelize outside the churches. In practice, however, churches are either ignored or stamped out.

CHURCH LIFE

Christianity first came to China via missionaries from the Middle East in A.D. 635. Christians in China have grown to an estimated sixty to eighty million members today. Church life is marked by paradox: though it is rich, vibrant, filled with renewal, and growing at a rapid pace, it is also persecuted, under-trained, and severely lacking in resources. An estimated fifty million Christians in China are still waiting for their first Bible, and without their own copy of the Scriptures many fall prey to heresy and false teaching. Many evangelists are zealous, but the vast majority are poorly trained and ill-equipped. There are conflicts between leaders, and many feel the worst temptation faced by the church is materialism, particularly in the context of China's exploding economy.

PERSECUTION

The goal of the government is stability and control; this is the motivation behind population control, economic reform, and religious management. Its religious policy is one of control and repression. The Three Self Patriotic Movement (commonly called the Three Self Church) is the "registered" church, closely governed by the Communist Party, and the government has launched sporadic crackdowns on the unregistered house churches. Persecution is dependent mainly on whether the government perceives danger from the religious group. Some observers believe the Chinese government's greatest fear is that pro-democracy activists and religious activists will link with the disaffected unemployed, whose numbers are rising rapidly. Christians are not singled out for persecution; Muslims and Buddhists have, in some instances, received harsher treatment than Christians have, and many smaller sects and religious groups have been regularly stamped out of existence. Christian persecution ranges from fines and Bible confiscation to destruction of house church buildings; evangelists have been arrested, beaten, tortured, interrogated, imprisoned, and some have died as a result of this treatment. Aside from government persecution, Christians attempting to evangelize Muslims in China's northwest corner have met with resistance and some persecution. Buddhists in the former Tibetan region have been more organized about their resistance to the inroads of Christianity.

In late 1998, Ah King, a female house church leader in northeast China, had just finished expounding her text to her congregation when Public Security Bureau officials whisked her away and threw her into a freezing cell. Her interrogator, Wu Pei Fu, was the head of the Public Security Bureau in the area. For some reason he took an instant dislike to Ah King, and instead of using more subtle psychological techniques, he began to beat and kick her. "Tell me who the other leaders are! Who supplies your Bibles?" He screamed questions, and when she refused to answer, he would rain more blows upon her.

But Christians were praying, and Wu was in for a shock. He interrogated Ah King for only twenty-four hours, but the hours were full of surprises for the brutal official. First, he heard his mother was in the hospital as the result of a bad car accident. Next, news came that his son was very sick with a stomach ailment. Finally, when he went home, he had a fierce argument with his wife, who threatened to leave him.

In the morning Wu took his frustration out on Ah King, beating her repeatedly and then sending word to her congregation: "If you don't pay RMB 20,000 for her release, I will send her to a labor camp for three years." The sum was exorbitant (nearly U.S.$2,500). The congregation could not afford to pay, since in the area the average yearly salary was less than half that amount. But they prayed, and a contact in another city agreed to raise the money. Ah King was released.

Hearing that her interrogator's mother was ill, Ah King went straight to the hospital to see her. She located the mother, who was lying on the bed, her other son in attendance, and began witnessing to her. She preached the gospel to her and then sent word to the other Christians. They all came and prayed at the bedside, and in a matter of hours the mother and her son had both trusted Christ. The Christians also prayed for Wu's wife and son. The son was healed. Wu was amazed at the boldness and the effectiveness of the Christians, and when his mother started attending the house church of Ah King, whom he had so badly abused, he made no objection.

THE FUTURE

Persecution and restrictions have been unable to stop the church and only barely to slow it. It is generally believed that by 2050 the church in China will number well over one hundred million believers, and with further openness could become one of the most significant forces for evangelism in the world. Once the barriers to travel are lowered enough for Chinese to venture freely abroad, the Chinese church could become one of the biggest mission-sending bases of all time.

PRAYERS FOR THE SUFFERING

1. *The church is enduring growing pains.* Praise God for the enormous growth of the church. Pray that persecution will be lightened, training materials will be provided, and Bibles will be made available in order to stanch heresy.

2. *Chinese Christian leaders bear much for the sake of the gospel.* Pray for the thousands of Chinese evangelists and pastors who endure sleepless nights, separation from their families, secret meetings, and the possibility of arrest

in order to shepherd their flocks. Many are ill-equipped and have little training, yet travel from place to place to share what they know.

3. *The expanding economy is regarded as one of the greatest trials of the church*. Persecution is considered a blessing by Chinese Christians. The main worry of Chinese pastors is the effect of materialism caused by China's growing economy. Pray that the church will not lessen its fervor in the wake of materialistic temptations.

4. *Many pastors have been consigned to labor camps*. Food is poor and work is harsh, but many have been able to preach and form churches within the camps. Some have been so effective that they have been placed in solitary confinement to keep them from preaching.

5. *The church suffers from a sharp lack of unity*. Many leaders in the Three Self Patriotic Movement (TSPM) and the unregistered house churches fear and distrust each other. Some accuse the TSPM of selling out, while TSPM leaders believe house churches are sinning by acting against the government. Pray that the divisions between them will be healed and the leaders will be reconciled.

6. *China suffers from a lack of Bibles*. This remains one of the most significant needs. Although there are tens of millions of Christians in China, very few have their own copy of the Bible. Some have never even seen a copy. The result can be unintentional heresy. Pray that more Bibles will be made available to Chinese believers.

7. *China also suffers from a lack of evangelistic resources*. Praise God for the many varieties of evangelistic tools that are brought into the country each year. Tracts and videos all result in numerous converts per copy distributed. Pray that the number of resources brought into the country will be increased.

Please Pray for the Persecuted Church in:

COLOMBIA

POPULATION	**PERSECUTION**
40 million (73% urban)	Isolated, static
LAND	**RESTRICTIONS & FREEDOMS**
Northern South America;	Freedom of worship
440,831 sq. miles	Freedom to change religion
(1,141,748 sq. km)	Freedom to evangelize
LANGUAGE	**IN THE 21ST CENTURY...**
Spanish	Ongoing opposition from
	drug lords and guerrillas
RELIGION	will spark incidents of vio-
97% Christian	lence against Christians.
CHRISTIANS	
34 million, share static	

Located in Latin America, Colombia is marked by dense jungles and a tropical atmosphere. It is well-known for two products: coffee and cocaine.

Colombia's forty million people are nearly all Spanish-speaking Mestizos, Europeans, and Mulattos; there is a small minority of Amerindians. Most are literate; nearly one-third are under the age of fifteen, and three-quarters live in cities. Bogota, the capital, is also the largest city with five million inhabitants.

Colombia obtained its independence from Spain in 1819 as part of Grand Colombia. It became a separate state in 1831. Political infighting, Marxist guerrilla warfare, and the industry of drug lords have combined to create more than a century of civil unrest and warfare. New elections in 1991 were held in the hope of seeing peace.

Colombia has had a money-laundering law since 1995, but no one has been convicted under the statute; worse, drug lords have adapted to pressure from the government and replaced their ostentatious lifestyles with more low-key ones. They have become virtually unknown yet very efficient, dealing in an estimated five hundred and fifty tons of cocaine yearly.

Coupled with this is the problem of warfare; Colombia has one of the longest-lasting guerrilla conflicts in the Western hemisphere. Between 1990 and 1994, armed insurrection did more than $12.5 billion in damage and killed some seventeen thousand people; the military spends one-third of the national budget on its battle against insurgents. Many rebels are young: one-tenth of their ranks is composed of teens from thirteen to seventeen years old. Many of these guerrillas finance their activities through the drug trade.

With the inability of the government to conquer or even stem the tide of warfare, paramilitary forces (private armies) have spread rapidly and changed from defensive to offensive postures. They continue to strengthen and successfully carry out operations against guerrilla strongholds and are active mainly in areas lacking any police or military protection.

In all this, Colombia's civilians are the losers. The nation has been deeply marked by unrest and is known to be one of the most violent in the world. Three murders occur every hour—roughly seventy-one per day, almost twice as many as in the whole of Europe. Some 45 percent of the world's kidnap-

pings occur in Colombia. In spite of this situation, only one in two hundred crimes receives due punishment. The victims are usually very young: 47 percent of Colombia's children have been abused by violence. It is estimated that Colombia's internal warfare costs the country at least U.S.$3.2 billion yearly. Paramilitary groups have forced thousands of peasants to leave their lands in order to clear the field for battle, creating a huge exodus of displaced people who have moved into the cities—where a new cycle of poverty and violence begins.

Colombia is a republic with a democratic constitutional government. The president is elected by popular vote for a four-year term and no reelection is allowed. The main political parties are the Liberal, the Social Conservative, the Democratic Alliance/M-19, and the Patriotic Union. Andrés Pastrana was elected president in 1998.

Colombia is dominated by the Catholic Church. A small minority (about 2 percent) are nonreligious, or atheists. Some of the Amerindian tribes still hold to their traditional religions, and there are small pockets of Muslims, Baha'is, and Jews.

CHURCH LIFE

The first Catholic diocese was established in Colombia in 1534; the first Protestant missionaries arrived in 1825. Today Protestants make up about 4 percent of the country and Catholics some 93 percent. In 1953 a "missions treaty" gave Catholic missionary orders exclusive rights of evangelism in the nation, denying any such role to Protestants. This was later ended, and in 1991 the new constitution went so far as to take away the Catholic Church's position of privilege in the society and grant greater freedom to religious minorities.

Despite the wrangling between the traditions, Christianity continues to be a significant force in the life of Colombia. Aggressive evangelism has helped the church to grow even more. Recent research indicates that the country's instability has caused many Colombians to reevaluate their religious beliefs, bringing forth a new fear of God, whatever their creeds are. Even guerrillas are being reached with the gospel; a good number of them who have deserted and have given their lives to Jesus are now very determined to bring the Word of God to everyone around them, especially their former comrades.

PERSECUTION

Church growth has been significant. Guerrilla groups, drug cartels, corrupt government bodies, and traditional religions continue to test the faith of new believers. Converts are branded as traitors, and some have been targets for assassination. Missionaries have been threatened, kidnapped, and sometimes murdered. Many Christians have been martyred for their stand against crime.

Crime is so bad that paramilitary groups, endorsed by police officials, use violence to counter violence. At a very young age, Fausto, along with his brothers Caleb and Mario, joined one such group. The desire to have power by the use of arms was the motivation of these siblings to create terror within the city of Bogota. For years they participated in violence. They executed all who they said collaborated with some type of guerrilla movement. They called this "cleansing" and even paid police officials a service fee to allow them to participate in their planned activities.

One day Fausto met the Lord Jesus and learned of His love for all of them. He was transformed into a true soldier of God's heavenly army. His testimony had such an impact that it led to the conversion of all his brothers, including Caleb and Mario.

Fausto's preaching focus was his old companions in crime. He and his brother

Caleb distributed more than one thousand Bibles among members of the guerrilla groups and paramilitaries. This led many to accept Jesus Christ. However, it also awakened unease among those who saw their ranks decrease because so many lives were changed by the gospel. In the fall of 1999 an armed group attacked and shot indiscriminately at Fausto's house. Miraculously no family member was hurt. However, a few days later a note was pushed under the door in which they threatened death to all the family, especially Fausto, if they did not leave the city.

Fausto moved to a rural area, where he continued his ministry to one hundred and fifty people who had relocated to the small town to escape violence. Not long after, his brother Mario was assassinated. The same morning his brother Caleb was selling cakes in a small plaza when he heard some men call him by a nickname he used when he belonged to the paramilitary force. He showed no reaction to the name, and then he heard someone in the group say, "I don't think that is him."

That evening several armed men arrived at Fausto's house and ordered him to come with them. They told his wife that she would see him the following day. Fausto's wife and children began to cry and to ask the men not to take him. They ignored their pleas and took him into the bush. With no electricity on the property, it was very dark, and some of his children followed. They witnessed their father being struck repeatedly and heard him say, "You are mistaken. I am a child of God." When the men realized they were being followed, they put Fausto in a car and took him away. Hours later Brother Fausto was found dead. His hands were tied and his body showed signs of torture. With him was his bag with his Bible and leaflets he used when he preached.

THE FUTURE

The Protestant church is currently growing at about double the rate of the Catholic Church but is unlikely to gain a significant share of the population any time soon. Although Christianity has a firm position in society, it has so far failed to see an end to the severe violence and crime that permeates the land. The hope is that the beginning of the end will be seen soon.

PRAYERS FOR THE SUFFERING

1. *The church has suffered terribly at the hands of the drug trade.* Pray for a major evangelistic penetration of the drug industry, with cartel leaders coming to faith in Christ and abandoning the illegal trade.

2. *The nation as a whole has been wounded by violence and crime.* Pray for a Christian revival to permeate the country and see a lessening in tensions.

3. *Evangelists and Christian leaders have been threatened and killed.* Pray for their protection from drug lords and guerrillas and for their continued boldness to proclaim the gospel.

4. *Missionaries have been kidnapped and held for months and years.* Pray for the protection of those who work in Colombia and for the release of Christians who have been held by guerrilla groups.

COMOROS ISLANDS

POPULATION
592,000 (31% urban)

LAND
Southeastern Africa islands;
863 sq. miles (2,235 sq. km)

LANGUAGES
Arabic, French, Comoran

RELIGION
98% Muslim

CHRISTIANS
7,000; share growing

PERSECUTION
Sharp, static

RESTRICTIONS & FREEDOMS
No public meetings

IN THE 21ST CENTURY...
Sporadic intense persecution will be coupled with general restrictions that impede the growth of the church.

The Comoros Islands are four volcanic islands located between the continent of Africa and the island of Madagascar, near the island of Mayotte. The terrain is extremely rocky and poor agriculturally, although the sea life is rich and varied.

Most of the people are Comorians, of mixed Arab, African, and Malagasy heritage. It is split nearly evenly between male and female; almost half are under the age of fifteen, and a third live in urban areas, which are growing in size at a remarkable rate.

The Portuguese first discovered the Islands in 1503, but France arrived and took them in 1517. They became a French protectorate in 1886 and remained such until 1961 when they were granted internal autonomy. In 1975 they formed a republic and declared themselves independent. Mayotte was one of its possessions, but at that time it seceded to remain a French territory. The island remains disputed. Since independence numerous coups have been attempted; a multiparty democracy was established in 1990.

The Islands remain underdeveloped and poor. The economy is stagnant; most of the populace are subsistence farmers and fishermen. The Comoros Islands is the world's largest perfume oils producer and second largest vanilla producer, but collapsing global prices in both these markets have left the islanders with little income. The average worker earns less than U.S.$500 per year; about half are literate and most live to be sixty. A quarter of the children under the age of five suffer from malnutrition.

The Islands were settled by Arabs early in the fourteenth century and Islamicized in the fifteenth century. Most Muslims are Sunnis of the Shafiite rite. There are hundreds of mosques and Qu'aranic schools, and the regular annual pilgrimage to Mecca takes about a hundred people yearly. A small minority of a few hundred Baha'is lives on the Islands as well.

CHURCH LIFE

Catholics came to the Comoros with the French in the 1500s. Today there are about seven thousand believers, most of whom are French, Malagasy, or Reunionese; there are thought to be less than two hundred indigenous Comorian believers. Most of the Christians are Catholics but about a quarter are Protestants. The Africa Inland Mission has had substantial work on the Islands, which has earned the respect and favor of the populace. While the Comorian church has remained small, it has continued to grow.

PERSECUTION

African Christian leaders say these Islands are the world's most difficult to evangelize. The government does not acknowledge any indigenous Christians and does not permit believers to meet openly. Believers cannot express their faith in public for fear of arrest. Open Christian witness is completely forbidden, though quiet house meetings have been held. Persecution has been periodic and sporadic but intense; this pattern does not appear to be changing.

On the island of Anjouan, a group of about twenty-five young Christian men who had a real interest in reaching out to young people ran into problems when spies reported their intentions. A Muslim prayer leader visiting from Egypt told local authorities that they should either kick the Christians out of the village or have them all live together in some isolated corner. The imam's assertion caused a dispute in the village: some said the Christians should be beaten, some suggested they should be expelled from the town, others wanted to confiscate their books, and some of the imams felt that they should be left alone. There were also people in the village who supported the Christians.

New problems erupted in April 1999 when the village people heard of twenty-nine-year-old Antoine's baptism. People driving by witnessed it and passed on the news to others. The villagers didn't know how to respond. First they wanted to call the young man to the mosque for discipline. Then they decided Christians could not be involved in Muslim affairs. Some determined they would secretly call the Embargo—a group of local militia.

Antoine was arrested early on a Saturday morning by two Embargoes; two others were taken from a school. Antoine, Jean, and Thibault were taken to a makeshift prison in Pomoni, where they were beaten with batons and thick electrical wires. People of the village, including Antoine's uncle, paid money for their release. Antoine was released first and told to turn over his Christian books. The Embargoes accompanied him to his home, but he didn't allow them into his room. He hid *When Persecution Comes* and brought out the other books and his New Testament. Jean and Thibault were released later that day and then called to appear at the local police station, where they were threatened with beatings unless they signed a statement renouncing their faith.

THE FUTURE

The growth of the church is outpacing that of the general population, and it is likely that the total number of believers in the Islands could reach more than 60,000 by 2050. Persecution will probably continue to be sporadic, yet sharp.

PRAYERS FOR THE SUFFERING

1. *Believers suffer from the poverty of the nation.* Travel, evangelism, and church planting can be difficult for the local church, lacking evangelistic resources to implement major programs. Pray that the church around the world will help equip the Comorian church for evangelism.

2. *The church enjoys a tolerant atmosphere.* Although there are restrictions on its activities, Christians in general have a fairly good reputation on the Islands, and cases of persecution remain isolated. Pray that the church will continue to earn the respect and favor of the country.

3. *The church suffers from an inability to proclaim the gospel openly.* Pray that the government will soften its restrictions and permit open meetings and the celebration of Christian holidays.

4. *The nation has been hurt by political turmoil.* Pray that the church will be able to conduct a ministry of healing and reconciliation on the Islands.

Please Pray for the Persecuted Church in:

CUBA

POPULATION 11.2 million (76% urban)	**PERSECUTION** Harassment, declining
LAND Caribbean island; 42,804 sq. miles (110,861 sq. km)	**RESTRICTIONS & FREEDOMS** Freedom to worship Evangelism is restricted Growing freedoms for the church
LANGUAGE Spanish	**IN THE 21ST CENTURY...** There will likely be contin-
RELIGION 44% Christian, 30% non- religious, 25% spiritist	ued growth in personal freedom and correspond- ing explosive church
CHRISTIANS 4.5 million, share growing	growth, particularly among house churches.

The largest island in the Caribbean, Cuba lies some ninety miles off the coast of Florida. The terrain is split fairly evenly between forested and farmed areas.

Cuba's eleven million people are largely young and urban. Although just 20 percent are under the age of fifteen, more than 60 percent are under the age of forty-four. Havana, the island's capital, is the largest city with more than two million residents. Most Cubans are Spanish-speaking Whites, but there are minority groups of Asian expatriate workers.

The Republic of Cuba is a Communist state. The current government assumed power on January 1, 1959. The nation has only one political party, the Cuban Communist Party (PCC). A totalitarian state, Cuba is under the rule of Fidel Castro, who acts as president of the council of state and council of ministers, commander-in-chief of the armed forces, and first secretary of the Cuban Communist party. The government has full control of the electronic and the print media. Under the Communist system, Cuban citizens do not have the right to freely choose their government representatives, equal protection under the law, freedom of expression, freedom to travel to and from the island without restriction, or freedom of peaceful assembly and association.

The government of Fidel Castro has turned the Cuban society into one of the most highly militarized in the world. With the exception of Brazil, Cuba has the largest and perhaps the most modern military in Latin America. This power, however, has been greatly diminished by the collapse of the former Soviet Union; the shortage of fuel, spare parts, and other materials has sharply reduced training and military exercises.

Young Cubans, however, generally do not remember Castro's revolution, and most are less interested in political ideology than in economic growth. Nearly all are literate, but poor: the average Cuban earns around U.S.$2,000 yearly; the economy has been devastated by years of embargo, centralized planning, and the collapse of the Soviet Union. Except for tourism, Cuba has had limited success in attracting foreign investors because of the deterioration of the economy, its unpaid debt to Western countries, and the lack of clear titles to expropriated property. Tourism has increased more than 20 percent annually for the last several years. However, there is still a deficit of over $1 billion dollars, according

ing to estimates of the Banco Nacional de Cuba in its May 1996 statement, in addition to the country's foreign debt, which around that time added up to U.S.$11 billion. Cuba's enormous old debt to the former countries of the Soviet Union is not included in these figures.

Although the Castro regime officially declared Cuba to be an atheistic state, the largest organized religion is still the Roman Catholic Church. Yet experts estimate that less than 5 percent of the island's population is practicing Catholic; out of 4.5 million baptized followers, only about 150,000 attend mass on a regular basis.

The Afro-Cuban syncretism Santería could be Cuba's main religion. Santería is an animistic belief based on the Yoruba religion brought by the African slaves during the Colonial era, which then mixed with Catholicism. It reckons that the African gods have a Catholic alter ego. Since Santería doesn't have an organized structure, it is hard to assess the number of its followers, but it is reported that at least 60 percent of Cubans have participated in a Santería ritual at one time or another. According to the number of baptisms, it is estimated that 35 percent of the Cuban population is Catholic, but this figure could be inaccurate, since all practicing santeros consider baptism to be an essential requirement for partaking in their ceremonies.

During the past decade, however, various Christian denominations have been rapidly growing in number, to the point that it is now hard to find a Cuban village without a Protestant church. Several hundred thousand people attend a church service on Sunday.

CHURCH LIFE

Catholic missionaries with the Dominican order arrived in 1512, soon after Columbus' landfall in 1492. The Roman Catholic Church has been firmly established in Cuba ever since, but church attendance has declined catastrophically since 1960. Although Catholics number 41 percent of the population, actual attendance is estimated at a mere 2 percent. Although the Protestant churches have been decimated by emigration to the United States, they have still experienced spectacular growth: a rate of 6 percent per year (as opposed to the Catholic growth rate of 2.4 percent).

PERSECUTION

In numerous documents and laws the government has clearly stated itself to be completely neutral on the subject of the church, demanding absolute separation of church and state and neither giving support to the church nor asking anything of it. In practice, severe restrictions on meetings, street evangelism, and church construction have made life difficult. Pastors have been arrested and imprisoned, churches have been infiltrated by informers, and discrimination is a constant way of life. Fortunately, today there is little real danger of martyrdom, and persecution is generally ending. Restrictions are still in evidence but a new openness has made wider ministry possible.

A 1992 amendment to the constitution changed the nature of the Cuban state from atheistic to secular, enabling believers to belong to the Cuban Communist Party. This, however, is yet to be fulfilled. Devout members of Christian and Catholic denominations usually face intense opposition and harassment by authorities.

The visit of Pope John Paul to Cuba in January 1998 is looked upon as a major breakthrough after decades of repression against all religious institutions. The effects of it, however, are still to be determined. While the world watched in awe at the multitudes participating in all the religious activities, government security agents visited several evangelical churches and demanded that the leaders cancel all evangelistic activities planned for the week of the Pope's visit. Obviously the attacks against the evangelical church haven't stopped. Agents demanded that the "house churches" be permanently closed down and that pastors sign a document indicating that such measures were strictly voluntary. As in the past, the pastors refused to do it, even though they risked being arrested and even exiled.

That's what happened to Dr. Eliezer Veguilla, who had two dreams as a young boy: to serve the Lord Jesus Christ faithfully and to become the best medical doctor in a country where few Christians have been allowed to enter top professional fields. Born into the home of the Reverend Leoncio Veguilla (one of the pastors imprisoned in 1965 along with more than fifty other pastors and missionaries), he graduated in 1981 as a medical doctor, specializing in internal medicine, intensive therapy, and geriatrics at the Salvador Allende Hospital of Havana.

Eliezer helped to distribute thousands of Bibles, New Testaments, and Christian materials to believers throughout the island. "We were once conducting a very special evangelistic campaign with the movie *Jesus*, which was scheduled to be shown at a rural church, where, in an effort to keep people from watching it, the police cut off the power. However, we had a small generator, and since the church was the only place that had power, the whole town came out and watched it."

One day Eliezer was arrested as he left work for home. His "crime" was being a Christian leader. He was held and interrogated for forty-seven days by state security agents—without formal charges—and endured various types of torture, such as being switched back and forth between below-freezing and painfully-hot chambers; having to sleep with two strategically placed firearms aiming at his bed; a mock execution; misinformation and false information regarding his family; and being awakened at all hours of the night for intense interrogations.

The authorities, unable to find any evidence to convict him, placed him under house arrest, which kept him from getting involved in any Christian activities. He and his family became the target of constant surveillance and threats by officials. Eighteen months later, Eliezer and his wife and two children were forced out of the country to live in the United States.

THE FUTURE

With the decline in persecution and the explosion of house churches and quiet, tactful support, the church is exploding in numbers. It is possible that Protestants will number well into the millions early this century. If complete openness comes to the country, the interactions between Protestants and Catholics may touch off a wide renewal and revival in both, sparking new initiatives to evangelize the nonreligious and spiritist elements of the society.

PRAYERS FOR THE SUFFERING

1. *The church is enjoying unprecedented revival.* Praise God for the massive revival that has permeated Cuba and for the explosive growth of the house churches. Pray that this expansion will be maintained.

2. *The church is enjoying a new day of freedom.* Praise God for the significant lessening in restrictions, and pray that this will continue. Thank God for the favor the government has recently shown to Protestant and independent house churches, and pray that this will improve.

3. *The church is enjoying substantial global support.* Thank God for the significant support network providing Bibles and other evangelistic resources to the house churches. Pray that this will be expanded.

4. *The church has the opportunity to permeate the nation with Christianity.* Pray that the country will continue to develop into a nation where there is broad freedom to evangelize and where churches may be widely planted.

Please Pray for the Persecuted Church in:

DJIBOUTI

POPULATION	**PERSECUTION**
630,000 (82% urban)	Harassment, growing
LAND	**RESTRICTIONS & FREEDOMS**
Eastern Africa; 8,958 sq.	Freedom of religion
miles (23,200 sq. km)	Freedom to evangelize
LANGUAGES	**IN THE 21ST CENTURY...**
French, Arabic, Somali,	Islam will continue to
Afar	maintain strong social
	barriers to Christian
RELIGION	evangelism.
95% Muslim	
CHRISTIANS	
30,000, share growing	

Djibouti is a hot, arid plateau on the northeast tip of the Horn of Africa. Its land is dotted with numerous saltwater basins and several mountain ranges, some of which are more than a mile high.

The country has more than half a million people, most belonging to either the Afar or Issa groups. There are minorities of Europeans and Arabs, many of whom are expatriate workers. A little less than half of the people are under the age of fifteen; Djibouti's population is growing fairly rapidly and is expected to double in thirty years. The capital city, also called Djibouti, is the largest city and home to more than 80 percent of the nation's people.

Djibouti is a poor country. The economy is dependent upon the capital, linked by railroad to Ethiopia, for which it also serves as a major seaport. The average worker earns less than U.S.$1,000 per year, and to make matters worse, Djibouti has an unemployment rate estimated at 40 percent.

The French came to Djibouti in the late 1850s, attempting to offset the English in Aden. In 1888 the country was made part of French Somaliland. Nationalistic fervor swept the country, but in a 1967 referendum the people voted to remain part of France. As a result, independence was postponed but finally granted in 1977. Hassan Gouled Aptidon was elected president at that time and ruled until 1999, when he stepped down and was replaced by his chief cabinet minister, Omar Ismael Guelleh.

Djibouti is nearly 95 percent Muslim, with the balance being Christian.

Islam came to the area in the twelfth century. Most are Sunnis, with a small minority of Shi'as. There is a very small contingent of Hindus among the Indian expatriate workers.

CHURCH LIFE

Catholic priests arrived in the late 1800s with the French, and the diocese of Djibouti was created in 1955. Protestant churches were first formed in the mid-1900s. Today there are several thousand Catholics and a smaller group of Protestants and Orthodox. Most of the Christians are expatriates and are served by several churches and other centers of worship.

PERSECUTION

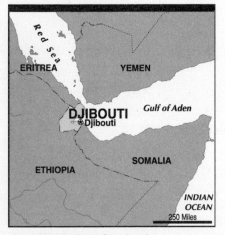

Although there is freedom of religion and freedom to evangelize, the Muslim majority is resistant to such activities. Converts to Christianity face many significant societal pressures. Recent trips into Djibouti by correspondents have uncovered many examples of discrimination and harassment.

"One evening our leader, the evangelist, led a prayer meeting at his home. About twenty Muslims forcibly entered the room and attacked the Christians with sticks and stones. The evangelist was stabbed in the leg with a knife. After beating him, they escaped, leaving him for dead.

"On another occasion we had prayers in our service room. The Djibouti State Police surrounded the room and entered without permission. They searched through the room and took documents, books, and some church materials. The men and women who attended the prayer group were arrested. At the station, a member of the police force beat one of the brothers with a metal bar. He was seriously wounded and almost died. He was taken to the hospital and remained there for a long time.

"As Paul and Silas had done in prison, the detained prayer group sang and rejoiced in the Lord. Witnessing this, some of the other prisoners joined them. Six of them accepted Jesus there in the jail. The group was released after three days.

"It is not only we who face persecution but also the Muslim converts. The community was incited against the converts and eventually they were excommunicated. They even lost their jobs. Now they have no food and shelter.

"There are also other cases of persecution. Generally the Lord Jesus Christ has taught us how to stand amid the suffering. He also taught us that He is close to us and will help us. He has kept us from fearing persecution.

"Dear Christian, pray that our God will encourage us and help us to reach the unreached for Him in Djibouti."

THE FUTURE

The concentration of the population in a single urban agglomeration and the lack of government-organized restrictions on evangelism combine to give the church a significant growth potential. Given current trends, it is possible Christians could triple in number by 2050. They will need to be supported with literature, training, and a variety of community development programs.

PRAYERS FOR THE SUFFERING

1. *The church enjoys broad freedoms.* Praise God for these and the growth they have sparked. Pray that the church will use this significant window of opportunity to broadly share the gospel.

2. *The church suffers from the hard societal barriers created by Islam.* Pray for increasing respect for the church and for Christians in Djibouti on the part of Muslims, and for social barriers to be softened.

3. *The church suffers from a lack of influence in the society.* Pray for the conversion of Djibouti leaders and prominent Muslims to Christianity; these conversions could be a significant Christian witness to the general populace.

4. *Believers suffer in the midst of Djibouti's poverty.* Pray for Christian organizations devoted to compassionate relief and development to find new opportunities to work in Djibouti.

Please Pray for the Persecuted Church in:

EGYPT

POPULATION 68.4 million (45% urban)	**PERSECUTION** Sharp, growing
LAND Northeastern Africa; 386,662 sq. miles (1,001,449 sq. km)	**RESTRICTIONS & FREEDOMS** Muslims may not convert Christians have different identity cards Converts may be arrested,
LANGUAGE Arabic	imprisoned, ostracized
RELIGION 84% Muslim	**IN THE 21ST CENTURY...** There will be numerous confrontations between
CHRISTIANS 10.3 million, share growing slowly	Christians and Muslims, with the government striving to keep peace.

E gypt is three times the size of New Mexico, and like that state, much of Egypt's land is desert. Only 3 percent is arable; most of this is found on the banks of the great Nile River. Egypt is strategically located on the Sinai Peninsula, the only land bridge between Africa and the European/ Middle Eastern hemisphere. Egypt also controls the Suez Canal, which is the shortest sea link between the Indian Ocean and the Mediterranean Sea.

Most of Egypt's citizens are Egyptians, but there are small minorities of other Middle Eastern peoples. Over a third of Egypt's inhabitants are under the age of fifteen. Cairo (fourteen million) and Alexandria (three million) are the two major cities.

The history of Egypt dates back before the Pharaohs of the Old Testament. Despite the hardship and slavery that Egypt placed on Israel in the years before Christ, they have in recent years played an important role in helping Israel obtain peace through the treaty of 1979. Egypt won their independence from the United Kingdom on February 28, 1922.

President Sadat's diplomacy (1970–81) ended the dominance of the former Soviet Union and won control of the valuable Suez Canal and Sinai oil fields from Israel as an outcome of the 1973 Yom Kippur War. The generally popular peace treaty with Israel in 1979 was bitterly opposed by many Arab nations, and Muslim extremists within the country, and led to Egypt's isolation in the

Middle East and Sadat's assassination. Since then, Egypt's political reforms have reinstated a multiparty democratic government. Currently Egypt's government is based on English common law, Islamic law, and the Napoleonic codes.

Egypt faced many economic problems at the end of the 1980s, including low productivity and poor economic management, compounded by the adverse social effects of excessive population growth. In the 1990s Egypt took sharp measures to address these problems, and they were able to release much of their debt under the Paris Club arrangements when joining with the coalition in the Gulf War. Unemployment remains high and tourism (a major source of income) has declined due to the 1997 massacre of foreign tourists at Luxor.

A large majority of the population is Muslim, and although Egypt is a sec-ular government, Islam is the state religion. Unfortunately, Islamic fundamen-talism grows with every economic setback; in 1992 the government was forced to crack down on extremists.

CHURCH LIFE

Christianity came to Egypt in the first century after Christ. Tradition says St. Mark founded the church of Alexandria. Many important Christian movements began in the years afterward. Islam came in the mid-dle centuries, and mass conversions brought Islam into the majority position it holds today. Christians make up about 14 percent of the population, but their share is growing very slowly, mainly through births to Christian households. Each year a number are lost to defections to Islam and to emigration out of the country.

PERSECUTION

Although Christians are permitted freedom of religion, it does not extend so far as the freedom to evangelize. New identity cards are issued for anyone who becomes a Christian. Muslims who convert are regarded as apostates. Converts suffer severe persecution, which can include social ostracism, arrest, and torture. Believers have reported campaigns by Islamic militants to system-atically force whole villages to convert to Islam. Muslim extremists have been known to kidnap Christian girls in a "convert-by-rape" tactic. Expatriate Christians can face harassment, arrest, and expulsion. Egypt's Coptic Christians (who are part of an ancient church in Egypt) have, in recent years, been increasingly persecuted as well: some have been murdered by radical militants and some have been required to pay "protection money." Permission must be obtained from the president to repair or construct church buildings.

Poor economic conditions in Egypt are putting extra pressure on the church. One Christian leader reports, "The situation I see around me often causes me great sorrow. In my town, which used to be completely Christian, the picture is changing daily. The majority of the people have become Muslim now; many of the Christians have emigrated or gone to larger cities in our country. Those who have remained very often live in a state of poverty."

Christians also have to cope with discrimination and humiliation because they are often considered second-class citizens. Many believers have left the city and have gone to rural areas. They find it easier to live there than to face oppression in the city every day. But living in the villages and in the fields, they are without any spiritual encouragement and teaching. They are too poor to provide a salary for a pastor, and many of the pastors have left rural areas to find employment in the larger cities.

"There are so many people who call themselves Christians who hardly know anything at all about the One whose name they bear," the leader said. "The majority have no Bible and no training; they have no Sunday school material, and there is no encouragement. There is hardly any material for the youth; no books, no teachers, no one who really cares for them. It is very easy for them to become influenced by Islamic doctrines and—sometimes enticed by material profit—to denounce their faith.

"God's mandate for us here in Upper Egypt is to 'strengthen the weak, bring back the strays, and search for the lost'—in short, take care of His flock. We try to do this through various means. First, we do this through our literacy classes. It is a very effective work and has brought many to a knowledge of Jesus Christ. Second, we have started to run a new system for Bible correspondence courses. Recently we had 700 students who joined us. Because so many churches in the villages have no pastor, we started a program to train lay leaders, who can carry responsibility in the communities. Training of these young men from the region is key not only for survival of the church but also for growth and outreach. We've also started to set up Bible study groups in the region. We move around from village to village, form small groups, and study the Bible and pray together once a week in someone's home.

"Because teenage girls are such a vulnerable group in our society, we have started organizing regular day conferences in which we cover a variety of subjects, such as dealing with fear—quite often they run the risk of being raped by Muslim boys and are then more or less obliged to marry them—dynamics in a Christian marriage, and the basics of our faith."

The Christian leader says he and other believers in rural areas are often harassed and threatened. They have had wild dogs sent after them and meeting places burned down. One building was set ablaze thirteen times.

"Sometimes all the activities and pressures get to me. The other day the security police called me in for questioning and wanted to know everything about my whereabouts. On top of that some of my family members tried to persuade me to emigrate to Australia. I must confess, I seriously considered it! My health is failing, the burden is heavy, and the going is tough. Then the Lord gently reminded me of Psalm 126:5: 'Those who sow in tears will reap with songs of joy.' I asked God whether someone else could please cry my tears for a while."

THE FUTURE

Egypt is likely to continue walking a thin line between conservatives and liberals. Although the government seeks to protect the Muslim faith, it must at the same time deal with extremists who might pose a threat to the stability of the government. Thus, Christians will continue to have an uneasy balance between freedom and insecurity. Although the church is adding members, its share of the population is presently in decline. By 2050 it may well have more than fifteen million members and yet comprise less than 13 percent of the population.

PRAYERS FOR THE SUFFERING

1. *The church benefits from a long history.* Pray that Egypt's Muslims will come to respect the ancient roots of the church and that the church will be permitted continued freedom of worship and increasing freedom to evangelize.

2. *The church is experiencing growth pains.* One of the fastest growing churches in Egypt is the house church movement—although some of these house churches are actually held in caves. Pray that the house church leaders will continue to plant new churches and raise up new leaders and evangelists.

3. *New believers face significant social persecution.* Pray for those who have converted to Christianity from Islam. They face significant societal pressures and threats and often must endure great loneliness and danger.

4. *Christians suffer from Egypt's economic difficulties.* Pray that Christians will find ways to serve Egypt with solutions for its problems. Pray that Westerners will find methods for assisting in this area as well.

Please Pray for the Persecuted Church in:

ETHIOPIA

POPULATION 62.5 million (16% urban)	**CHRISTIANS** Over 30 million, share growing
LAND Eastern Africa, landlocked; 446,953 sq. miles (1,157,603 sq. km)	**PERSECUTION** Sporadic, static
LANGUAGES Amharic, Tigrinya, Orominga, Guaraginga, Somali, Arabic	**RESTRICTIONS & FREEDOMS** Freedom to worship Freedom to evangelize
RELIGION 40% Orthodox 40% Muslim 14% Protestant	**IN THE 21ST CENTURY...** Current religious freedoms will continue to grow and persecution will diminish to very small levels; Ethiopia will be a strategic base for ministry in Sudan and Somalia.

E thiopia forms a major part of the eastern African land mass known as the Horn of Africa. It has a large number of mountains and plateaus divided by the Great Rift Valley, which runs southwest to northeast and is surrounded by lowlands and steppes. The land features tremendous diversity in climate and vegetation.

There are some sixty-two million people in Ethiopia, of whom about 16 percent live in the cities. More than one hundred ethnic groups are found in the land, and at least seventy languages are spoken as mother tongues. The largest group is the Oromo, which makes up about 40 percent of the population.

Ethiopia is the oldest independent country in Africa and arguably one of the world's oldest nations. There are over sixty references to Ethiopia in the Bible. Haile Selassie's imperial regime lasted from 1930 to 1974, with Italian occupation from 1936–41. Selassie was ousted by Communist Mengistu Haile Mariam, and the revolution established a Socialist state based on the principles of Marxism-Leninism, led by the Worker's Party of Ethiopia. Mariam ruled until 1991 when he was overthrown by the People's Revolutionary Democratic Front. Since mid-1991, a decentralized, market-oriented economy has been implemented to reverse economic decline. In 1993 gradual privatization of business, industry, banking, agriculture, trade, and commerce began. Yet another constitution was created and came into force in 1994. And in August 1995 Negaso Gidada was elected as president of the Federal Democratic Republic of Ethiopia.

A little more than 60 percent of the adults are literate following a major national literacy campaign. There are widespread health problems and major endemic diseases including malaria and tuberculosis. AIDS is becoming a tremendous problem. The average life-span in Ethiopia is fifty years old.

Islam and Christianity are becoming equal in strength. About 54 percent of the population is Ethiopian Orthodox and Protestant. Some 40 percent are Muslims, strongest in the north, east, and southeast. The remainder of the population practices various indigenous religions.

CHURCH LIFE

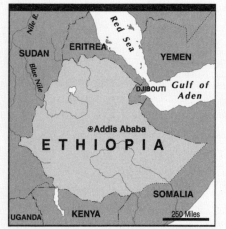

Tradition says a shipwrecked youth from Tyre brought Christianity to Ethiopia. The Ethiopian Orthodox Church dates its foundation to A.D. 332, and despite Islamic pressure in the seventh century, Ethiopia has remained dominated by Christianity throughout its history. The church numbers adds nearly one million members annually, most through births to Christian homes.

PERSECUTION

There was severe persecution during the Marxist regime of Mariam, but it has since slacked off enormously. The current atmosphere of freedom has contributed markedly to the enormous opportunity for evangelism, and both the national Ethiopian church and foreign missions are taking advantage of it. The year 1997 witnessed a strong rise in radical Islam as well as in Orthodox Christianity, both of which have united in their stance against "sheep-stealing" by evangelical groups. There has been a sharp rise in harassment and discrimination over the last few years. Here's the story of one Ethiopian believer:

"I was born into a family who practiced witchcraft, and they dedicated me to a spirit. When my mother passed away, exactly at that moment, I fell to the ground and became paralyzed on the left side of my body. I was also deaf in my left ear. An evil spirit told me to commit suicide. This spirit came to me where

I was sleeping and insisted that I should kill myself.

"One night I saw a vision. The vision looked like a fire that came from heaven. I looked at it in amazement. The fire descended onto our house, setting it ablaze, and finally it penetrated the house and stood behind me. The moment the fire was behind me, it looked like the Son of Man—a beautiful man. He started to speak to me. 'What did the evil spirit say to you?' He asked. I said, 'He said I should commit suicide.' The Son of Man said to me, 'You must not kill yourself; you will be my witness. From today on your left leg, your left hand, and left ear will be healed.' From that moment I was completely healed.

"After the incident I went to Addis Ababa and worked in the home of some relatives. My family in Addis belonged to the Coptic Church, and although they didn't read the Bible, they had one in their bookshelf. I took it and started reading the gospel of John in the New Testament. I wondered who this Jesus was whom I had never heard of before. As I was about to clean the room, I had another vision. The vision was of Jesus, the same Jesus I saw before. He said to me, 'You will be my witness; start going to church and accept me, for I am your Savior.' I cried and cried and cried. I became very afraid and considered myself a Pentie (derogatory name referring to a Pentecostal). *I have really become a Pentie. I don't want to be a Pentie*, I thought to myself. I fell asleep and all night long I heard the words: 'Jesus, Jesus, Jesus …' The next morning I went to the church and accepted Jesus as my personal Savior.

"The moment my family heard about this, they expelled me from the house, saying, 'If you've become a Pentie, you have betrayed us and we don't want to see you. Leave our house.'

"I went to a Christian who gave me food and shelter. This happened eight years ago. Since then I've been serving the Lord. In the name of Jesus, I will never go back to my old way of life.

"I recently went back to the village where I grew up and witnessed to five men. They don't have Bibles; I'm planning to go back there and give them some."

THE FUTURE

The church in Ethiopia is growing at a moderately fast rate and could see its numbers rise to more than one hundred million by 2050. If it can adequately resolve a pending confrontation with Islam, Christianity could come to permeate the whole of the nation.

PRAYERS FOR THE SUFFERING

1. *The church has suffered terribly but now enjoys a new era of freedom.* Praise God for this easing in tensions and the tremendous opportunity for new church growth and revival.

2. *Islam continues to challenge Christianity.* Pray for the church to adequately handle this with appropriate Christian responses of evangelism and church planting.

3. *Unity in the church remains a desirable goal.* Pray for the various groups within Ethiopia to unite together, reconcile with one another, and work together in the common goal of Christian evangelism.

4. *Ethiopia is home to large numbers of refugees.* Pray for the church to respond to refugee camps with service, support, aid, and love.

5. *Ethiopia is surrounded by many unreached people.* Pray for the Ethiopian church to further develop its missionary vision for the neighboring countries.

Please Pray for the Persecuted Church in:

INDIA

POPULATION	**PERSECUTION**
1.0 billion (27% urban)	Sporadic, growing
LAND	**RESTRICTIONS & FREEDOMS**
Southern Asia; 1,237,062 sq. miles (3,203,975 sq. km)	Freedom to worship Freedom to evangelize
LANGUAGES	**IN THE 21ST CENTURY...**
English, Hindi, Telugu, Bengali, indigenous	There will be continued conflict between radical elements of all the major religions present in India,
RELIGION	with continued Christian
82% Hindu, 12% Muslim	saturation of the south and moderate inroads
CHRISTIANS	into the north, the latter
30 million, share growing	accompanied by significant persecution.

India is the seventh largest country in the world, roughly one-third the size of the United States. Located in southern Asia, it is bordered on the north by the Himalayan foothills and the countries of Pakistan, China, Nepal, and Bhutan. A middle plains region is formed by three river systems: the Ganges, the Indus, and the Brahmaputra. The Deccan plateau is the southernmost and largest region of India.

India is second in world population with one billion inhabitants. By 2050 India will likely surpass China as the most populous nation with more than 1.5 billion people. Over one-third are under the age of fifteen, and nearly two-thirds are under the age of thirty. Many live in the cities: Greater Bombay is the largest, with more than fifteen million residents, but there are ten cities with more than one million. New Delhi is the capital of India's multiparty republic.

An Aryan invasion between 1500–1200 B.C. brought the beginnings of urbanization. In the sixth century B.C., Buddhism was born in the land. The first Hindu empire emerged in northern India around 321 B.C. The Muslim invasion began around A.D. 1000 and remained in power until the trading companies arrived on the scene. Most notably, the British East India Company took power and subdued the Muslims, controlling India from the 1750s. After World War I, Britain's influence dwindled, due in part to Gandhi's campaigns. A fully independent India was won in 1947. Hindus and Muslims were not united, however, and India was split into a mostly Hindu India and a Muslim Pakistan. Bad relations and disputed territory have erupted into border wars twice between the countries, and once with China.

India has an economy that impacts the world. Agriculture and industry are very important; diamonds, jewelry, and clothing are significant exports as well. Yet the average income per capita is U.S.$380, just 1.5 percent of what the average American makes. Some six hundred million live in deep poverty. With such a young population the government has struggled to provide adequate education, medicine, and nutrition for its people, and problems of illiteracy, disease, and infant mortality abound.

India has always been a very religious nation, and thousands of gods can

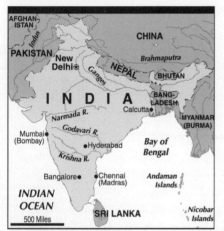

be found throughout the country. Hinduism claims the largest block of India's population, with 82 percent. Islam comprises 12 percent and Christianity 3 percent.

CHURCH LIFE

Of the more than thirty million Christians, some sixteen million are from Protestant or independent churches, and fifteen million are Catholics. There has been success in evangelizing despite a notably increasing trend in persecution. Nominalism is the biggest problem in the church—due in large part to the lack of discipleship training. Some of the best methods of evangelization are Christian radio broadcasts, which reach many with the Word of God. Indigenous Indian agencies and workers have been very successful as well. The India Missions Association coordinates over fifty evangelical agencies working in the country.

PERSECUTION

Government jobs and funds are withheld from converts, and surveillance of Christians is increasing. However, recent public cases of persecution of Christians has led to calls within the government for better protection of the rights and freedoms of believers. Most of the persecution has come from radical Hindus and Muslims, who have harassed, attacked, and even murdered Christians.

Christians in India welcomed the arrest of Dara Singh, alias Ravinder Kumar Pal, the mastermind behind the killing of Australian missionary Graham Staines and his two sons in January 1999. Singh was captured during an undercover police operation after eluding authorities for more than a year.

In a confession to police, Dara Singh said he wanted to teach Staines a lesson and not kill him. "I did not know that the young sons of Staines were there. I felt unhappy about their deaths. Staines was burned to death because this is a Hindu ritual," Singh reportedly told police.

Staines and his two sons were sleeping in a vehicle parked near the church in Manoharpur village in Orissa State when they were surrounded by a mob and burned to death.

Christians of the village have been living in constant fear ever since the ghastly incident. Two Christians, Rolia Soren and Chaitanya Munmi (pastor of the local church) have been asked not to go out alone at night.

Staines' wife, Gladys, said she was relieved at Dara Singh's arrest. "It is good. I am happy that he will not be able to kill others."

Richard Howell of the Evangelical Fellowship of India said, "We are happy that Dara Singh has been arrested. We hope that investigations into the case will continue and prove that the killing of Staines and his two sons was not an isolated incident but part of a larger agenda of hatred against the church by the Sangh Parivar (family of Hindu fundamentalist groups)."

Christians in India have expressed alarm over measures by the Orissa State government to further curtail religious freedom. Last year the Orissa government issued a memo to vigorously implement the Freedom of Religion Bill, which has been in effect there since 1967. The bill makes it mandatory for people who want to change their religion to inform the district magistrate, who will have the matter examined by the police. Conversion from Christianity to Hinduism is exempted from the bill.

Harold Mullick, a church leader in Calcutta, described the order as unconstitutional and discriminatory in nature: "It is a blatant violation of the freedom of religion guaranteed by the Indian Constitution."

THE FUTURE

The growth of the church has been met with negative responses from militant Hindus and Muslims, yet evangelism has continued to see fruit. It is likely that by 2050 Christians could number more than 250 million, or about 16 percent of the nation.

PRAYERS FOR THE SUFFERING

1. *The church enjoys a long history.* Praise God for the long-lasting impact of Christian missions in the nation. Pray that the indigenous Indian church will continue to strengthen its foundations and its evangelistic ability and further develop its missionary-sending capacity.

2. *The south has been saturated with the gospel.* Praise God for this. Pray that more missionaries and evangelists will work in the north, where there is more resistance and less evangelistic work.

3. *Christian workers in the north endure constant harassment and threats.* Pray for their protection and for God's provision for the many widows of martyrs.

4. *The church in India has been watered by the blood of the saints.* Pray that the martyrdom of Christians will be a substantial witness to Indians. Cases of Christian martyrdom are widely publicized throughout India, and many have come to faith in Christ as a result.

5. *Many Hindu radicals are deeply opposed to Christianity.* Pray for the softening of Hindu opposition to Christianity and for Christianity to gain favor with influential Hindu leaders.

Please Pray for the Persecuted Church in:

INDONESIA

POPULATION	**PERSECUTION**
212.1 million (36% urban)	Sporadic, growing
LAND	**RESTRICTIONS & FREEDOMS**
Southeastern Asian islands; 752,410 sq. miles (1,948,732 sq. km)	Freedom to worship Freedom to evangelize
LANGUAGES	**IN THE 21ST CENTURY...**
Bahasa Indonesia (Malay), English, Dutch, indigenous	There will likely be continued ethnic unrest and religious conflict
RELIGION	between Muslims and Christians, some of which
78% Muslim, 12% Christian	could become especially violent and warlike.
CHRISTIANS	
25 million, share growing	

Indonesia is located in southeastern Asia straddling a major sea-lane from the Indian Ocean to the Pacific. It is made up of some 17,000 islands, of which 6,000 are inhabited. The islands themselves are mostly coastal lowlands and interior mountains. Two-thirds of the terrain is heavily forested.

More than 212 million people live in Indonesia, making it home to the largest number of Muslims of any country in the world. One-third of the population is under the age of fifteen, and most will live to be sixty-two. Indonesia's population is broken into a number of ethnic groups, some of which have millions of members and most of which are unreached with the gospel.

The government of Indonesia is based on the Roman-Dutch law, which is modified by indigenous concepts and by the new criminal procedures code. Indonesia fought a very bitter and bloody battle with the Dutch for its independence, which was finally granted in December 1949. There is political freedom among the people that live in Indonesia.

Indonesia is a country that has been transformed by the production of steel, aluminum, and cement in 1965–1970. Today they are seen as having an unhealthy banking sector, untenable levels of private foreign debt, and uncompetitive practices that favored the financial interest of the former president and his friends. The labor force consists of about sixty-seven million while the unemployment rate is about 15 percent; most work in agriculture and manufacturing. About three-quarters of the population are literate. Primary school education is mandatory, and Indonesia is home to nine hundred universities.

About 78 percent of the population in Indonesia is Muslim, but there is a small number of Animists, Hindus, and Buddhists, and about 12 percent are Christian.

CHURCH LIFE

There are over twenty-five million Christians in Indonesia. The strong presence of Christianity continues to grow at better than 5 percent each year, adding more than one million converts annually. Despite the hostility against Christians and the radical actions of some groups, many Muslims are increasingly curious about Christianity and are free to accept copies of Scriptures.

PERSECUTION

The constitution recognizes the freedom to choose one's religion and fulfill one's religious obligations, and it guarantees liberty to evangelize so long as religious peace remains undisturbed. In reality, religious choice is confined to Islam, Protestantism, Catholicism, and Hindu-Buddhism. Churches may be built and courses given in schools; certain Christian holidays are even celebrated nationally. However, Muslims are clearly favored. State subsidies are used to sponsor Muslim teachers, mosques, and schools. Muslims have sometimes turned to violence, and mobs have destroyed Christian schools and churches. Anti-Christian fervor is often particularly felt in the densely Muslim areas such as Aceh, the northern tip of the island of Sumatra.

Further east, the Maluku Islands and the island-city of Ambon have been the scenes of recent sectarian clashes and riots. In early 1999, when the riots in Ambon started on the second day of the Idulfitri Muslim feast, fifteen-year-old Roy Pontoh became one of the youngest Christians to die for his faith in Jesus. Roy's classmates will not forget when Roy was singled out and questioned by Muslim assailants, "Who are you?" He replied, "I am a soldier of Christ." Hearing this, the perpetrators chopped off his left arm. With the intent to make the young boy deny his faith, they asked him again, "Who are you?" Having heard the same reply, the attackers did the same to his right arm. Unsatisfied, the men tried to force Roy to say, "Allahu Akbar." He only replied, "As far as I know, Jesus Christ is the only Lord." Right then and there they slashed open his stomach. Roy's last words were "I am a soldier of Christ."

Since then perhaps a thousand people or more have died in sectarian clashes on the Maluku Islands.

Although a number of Christian leaders and pastors have also become martyrs in the religious conflict that has shown no signs of abating until now, the death of Roy Pontoh was rather unique in that he was a young boy in his early teens and unwilling to deny his faith in the face of certain death.

The boy's remains were buried next to his home, but since the second wave of riots began again in July 1999, rendering almost two-thirds of the city of Ambon a complete ruin, the house was destroyed. The family has in the meantime moved to a remote town in Irian Jaya, where the father works in the forestry department.

THE FUTURE

The church is growing despite persecution. We can expect Christians in Indonesia to number more than sixty-five million by 2050. Over the next five decades it is likely that there will be recurring violence and tension between Muslims and Christians.

PRAYERS FOR THE SUFFERING

1. *The church has enjoyed a long history of peace.* For centuries Christians and Muslims have lived together in harmony. In the late 1990s this had begun to change as radicals attempted to incite sectarian violence. Pray that these tensions will be reduced and that reconciliation can be achieved.

2. *The church has enjoyed a substantial harvest.* Praise God for the growth of the Christian church. Pray for wisdom for Indonesian church leaders to evangelize, disciple, and train converts and commission them as evangelists.

3. *The church has enjoyed freedoms to worship.* Thank God for the enormous witness made possible by the construction of churches and schools and the national celebration of Christian holidays. Pray that the church will make wise use of these opportunities.

4. *The church has suffered in the midst of ethnic conflicts and religious tensions.* Indonesia has recently experienced large riots and religious warfare that have resulted in many deaths and significant economic damage. Widespread violence against the Christian minority, particularly in Java and Sumatra, has resulted in the killings of at least ten believers and the destruction of dozens of churches. Pray that these tensions will be eased and that Christians can serve Indonesia in a ministry of reconciliation.

Please Pray for the Persecuted Church in:

IRAN

POPULATION	**PERSECUTION**
67 million (60% urban)	Sharp, growing
LAND	**RESTRICTIONS & FREEDOMS**
Southwestern Asia; 630,578 sq. miles (1,633,189 sq. km)	No evangelism outside of churches
	Muslims may not convert
LANGUAGES	Muslims may not visit churches
Farsi, Turkish dialects, Kurdish	
	IN THE 21ST CENTURY...
RELIGION	The church will likely continue to be closely watched and heavily restricted, but existing substantial ministry partnerships will see much fruit.
99% Muslim	
CHRISTIANS	
300,000, share growing	

Iran is the modern name for ancient Persia, where many familiar biblical scenes were enacted—for example, Esther and Mordecai's struggle to save their people and Daniel in the lion's den. Iran is a large nation centrally located in the Middle East, with its deserts ringed by mountains.

About sixty-seven million people live in Iran, distributed among more than sixty ethnic groups. A large majority are Persians, but there are numerous groups with more than one million members each (notably the Qashqai, the Luri, the Kurds, and the Mazanderani). The population is split nearly evenly between urbanites and rural dwellers. Almost half are under the age of fifteen, and about three-quarters of the adults are literate. The population is growing rapidly and will double in size by 2025.

Iran has a long and ancient history. In the seventh century B.C., Cyrus the Great led the combined armies of the Medes and the Persians from Iran to forge one of the greatest empires the world has ever known. Darius continued to extend this empire until it stretched as far east as the Hindu Kush in Afghanistan. Alexander conquered the Iranian Empire and fused it with his own Greek force, but upon his death his domain was parceled out to his four generals. His empire was succeeded by the Sassanids, who restored Iranian culture and ruled until A.D. 640, when they were toppled by the Arabs of the Muslim armies. During the post-Mohammed schisms, Shi'a Islam became closely associated with Iran. The overwhelming invasion of the Mongol armies in 1200 devastated the country; much of the male population was killed and many large cities were destroyed. Iran had barely recovered when Tamerlane's armies swept through, albeit more slowly, and leveled such cities as Shiraz and Esfahan. The Safavid Empire came to power in 1501 after the disintegration of Tamerlane's Empire, ruled until 1720, and were followed by the Qajars, who ruled until the early 1900s. Political turmoil and attempted reforms were interrupted by the battle-grounds of World War I and World War II. In 1962 Mohammad Reza Shah came to power and attempted a broad set of reforms and modernization. Ultimately his reforms led to his downfall at the hands of conservatives. Ayatollah Khomeini took control in 1979 after toppling the government, and Iran has remained a

theocracy to this day. Since Khomeini's death, the new government has attempted to remain theocratic while moving more toward the middle.

The economy is largely based on oil. Although Iran made significant progress under the Shah, that progress was largely reversed in the decades following the 1979 revolution. Wars with Iraq further devastated the economy; today the average Iranian earns about U.S.$1,000 per year. Peace and increasing openness to the world is bringing some economic openings and improvements, but the rapid population growth is eroding the standard of living.

The government is a theocratic Islamic Republic. In recent years the government has become more moderate and less confrontational with the West. Nevertheless, despite this openness it continues to be closed internally and employs a secret police force to root out any dissent with little regard for freedom. The government is eagerly working to establish influence over Central Asia and in this respect considers Turkey its rival.

The state religion is Shi'a Islam. Muslims make up 99 percent of Iran's population. There is a small minority of Baha'is, Jews, and Christians.

CHURCH LIFE

There are 300,000 Christians in the nation, totaling less than one-half of one percent of the country. Most are Armenian Orthodox, but there are also several thousand in the Protestant and Roman Catholic traditions. The majority have come out of Christian families; converts from Muslim backgrounds number less than 10,000.

PERSECUTION

Restrictions and persecution have grown sharply in recent years. Christians from every tradition have been martyred; the Episcopal Church, which has the largest number of converts out of Islam, has suffered in particular. Although the rights of Christians, Jews, and Zoroastrians have been guaranteed by the constitution, in practice all have felt harassment. Church pastors have been arrested and detained, and in a few cases executed. Muslim converts are routinely interrogated and beaten. Moreover, many murders and assassinations have never been resolved but are widely believed to be the handiwork of radicals who regularly threaten Christian leaders with death.

Recent prominent martyrs include the Reverends Mehdi Dibaj, Tateos Michaelian, and also Haik Hovsepian Mehr, who was killed in January 1994. His widow, Takoosh Hovsepian, lives in Austria now, where she is waiting for a permit to migrate to the United States. There she will be reunited with the rest of her family. A worker from Open Doors-Holland visited her.

"I am so glad I can say thanks for all the cards and letters I received in the past five years," Takoosh smiled. "They have meant so much to me. Every time I read, 'I pray for you,' a bit more of my pain was taken away from me. The first months after Haik's martyrdom were especially difficult. We knew he was in a good place, but as a husband and father we missed him so much. Praise God, we were comforted by the Holy Spirit, and other Christians didn't leave us alone."

Takoosh told how God asked her to forgive her enemies. "Once a sister came to me and said that I had to forgive my husband's assassins. I answered that this was impossible for me. Then she said that I just had to pray for it. So I started praying, only with my mouth, for the forgiveness of my enemies. But later, through the power of the Holy Spirit, I learned to pray this prayer with my heart. I didn't know that I still had another step to take. The Lord showed me that I had to praise Him under all circumstances. Again I thought He asked the impossible and again He helped me to obey His order. Forgiveness is not enough. We must know that our God is the King of Kings. He is in control. We just have to praise Him under all circumstances."

When asked about the situation of the church in Iran, Takoosh hesitated. "You know, I'm still afraid to talk about it," she admitted. "Let me tell you this: the church in Iran still needs your prayers. Persecution continues, and the believers are under a lot of pressure. But also do thank the Lord that there are so many spiritually thirsty people. There are no empty churches in Iran! And if you are, for example, wearing a cross, people ask you about it. Please pray for the Christian believers and pastors in Iran. And pray for my family, that the Lord will use us everywhere we go."

THE FUTURE

Christian missions are not permitted in the land; most individual missionaries work "underground." Substantial partnerships have developed with a mission to evangelize Iran, gathered around both the Arabs and some of the minority peoples. Christian media are smuggled in and aired via satellite and shortwave radio, and some parts of the Iranian church are vigorous in evangelism. The church is growing and will likely have more than one million members by 2050, but compared with the overall population, it is still small and unlikely to form a substantial share of the country within the century.

PRAYERS FOR THE SUFFERING

1. *Growth brings the church new members and new persecution.* Praise God for the tens of thousands of Christians in Iran. Pray that Iran's church will be able to find creative, discreet ways to increase its growth rate through evangelism. Literature, videos, and Bibles have all been successfully distributed. Videos are often available on the black market, and animated gospel programs have been particularly appealing.

2. *Iranian church leaders have been martyred.* Pray for protection for Iranian Christians, particularly for leaders who have been harshly targeted in the past. Many have been martyred, and other leaders often battle personal fear.

3. *Many of Iran's martyrs had families.* Pray for the widows of the martyrs, who are left with their children and little means of support.

4. *The church looks with hope to moderation.* Pray for increasing liberalization in Iran, which may lead to better relations between Iran's Muslims and Christians.

5. *The populace resort to contraband to hear the gospel.* Secret satellite TV receivers are widespread despite their being illegal. Pray for fruit to result from satellite broadcasts blanketing Iran.

6. *Many of the minorities remain untouched by the gospel.* Pray for the mission teams that have adopted these groups and for the Iranian church to develop a vision for them as well.

Please Pray for the Persecuted Church in:

IRAQ

I raq is a largely desert country in the Middle East bordering Saudi Arabia, Turkey, and Iran. It can be divided into four major regions: deserts in the west, a rolling land between the upper Euphrates and the Tigris, highlands in the north, and an alluvial plain in the southeast.

Iraq has some twenty-three million residents. At its present growth rate, it will double in size around 2025. A slim majority are Iraqi Arabs; other minorities include the Kurds, Azerbaijanis, and Arabs from other nations. Arabic is the official language.

POPULATION
23.1 million (75% urban)

LAND
Southwestern Asia; 169,235 sq. miles (438,317 sq. km)

LANGUAGES
Arabic, Kurdish, Assyrian, Armenian

RELIGION
96% Muslim

CHRISTIANS
310,000, declining sharply

PERSECUTION
Isolated, growing

RESTRICTIONS & FREEDOMS
Constitutional freedom of religion
Freedom to change religion
Freedom to worship
Freedom to evangelize

IN THE 21ST CENTURY...
Limited freedom will continue to be enjoyed, and Iraq could be a significant discreet base for ministry throughout the Middle East while the secular regime remains in power.

At one time Mesopotamia, which encompassed present-day Iraq, formed the center of the Middle East and the civilized world. The ancient Sumerians used the fertile land and abundant water supply in the area to develop a highly complex society. Their successors, the Akkadians, crafted the Code of Hammurabi, the most complete legal system of the period. Located at the strategic heart of the ancient Middle East, the land was "a plum sought by numerous foreign conquerors," including the Assyrians and Chaldeans (who created the Hanging Gardens of Babylon). They were conquered by Cyrus the Great in 539 B.C., whose successors held the land but paid little attention to it until the Arab conquest and the coming of Islam in the seventh century. Iraq moved from ruler to ruler—the Mongols, the Ottoman Turks, and the British after World War I. The latter placed a king on the throne of Iraq, but a military revolution in 1958 overthrew him and led to the installation of the Ba'ath party and the Provisional Constitution of 1970.

The Constitution vested executive and legislative powers in the Revolutionary Command Council, whose chairman is also president of the country. There is a parliament called the National Assembly, which generally meets twice each year. The political system remains firmly under the control of the Ba'ath party. They granted the Kurdish minority a degree of autonomy but not the complete self-rule desired, and tensions and civil unrest have continued since. Iraq has been a prominent political force in the Middle East and has fought several wars with its neighbors, including numerous conflicts with Iran. Iraq's internal security force monitors dissidents.

Iraq is best known for oil, which makes up more than a third of its economy, but manufacturing and services actually contribute nearly half of the total economic output of the nation. The current regime has worked hard in the past to improve the standard of living but has squandered much of its wealth on wars. Education in public schools is free and there are several universities, but still it is estimated that less than 60 percent of adults are literate. Although health care has made rapid strides, diseases such as influenza and measles continue to afflict the nation, and there is an ongoing shortage of medical personnel (particularly in the rural areas and among the Kurds).

Roughly 96 percent of Iraqis are Muslims. Christians are the largest minority, estimated at about 3 percent of the nation. There are smaller minorities of nonreligious, atheists, Baha'is, and Jews.

CHURCH LIFE

Although Christianity continues to gain members, its share of the population is in a slow decline. Catholics have the largest block of Christians, but their 270,000 members represent a decline over the past two decades. Smaller groups such as the Orthodox and independent evangelicals have exhibited rapid growth.

PERSECUTION

Iraq's secular government restricts the activities of Christians yet permits them a greater degree of freedom than many other Middle Eastern nations. Ministries of compassion are permitted to bring humanitarian relief into the nation, and literature distribution has been a particularly fruitful ministry. Christians have a clear window in which to evangelize and minister, yet dangers exist.

Many believe Mansour Hussein Sifer was killed for his faith. The forty-three-year-old Christian convert from Northern Iraq was shot to death in April 1997. Mansour worked in a Christian bookshop in Arbil. A bold Christian, Mansour converted from Islam in 1995.

Mansour was last seen alive by his brother-in-law that fateful morning as he left home for the bookshop. At around 10:40 A.M. Mansour's co-worker found him dead, lying in a pool of blood. A close friend noted, "We found his New Testament on the floor beside him. He always had it with him, so I think he was pulling it out to speak about Jesus with whoever had come to kill him."

Mansour's young widow was left with a young boy, and after the death of her husband she found that she was pregnant. She has subsequently given birth to another son and continues to work for the Lord.

In November 1998, Open Doors had the opportunity to meet with Ruth Hussein in Northern Iraq, and she shared the following items for prayer:

"I praise God, because all my needs are being met. I really want to thank all the believers everywhere that they remember me in their prayers and for caring for us through sending cards and letters.

"I thank God for my children, Danny (1) and his brother Kevin (3). Pray for them and pray for me, as I am responsible for them. Pray that the Lord will make me strong and healthy (after her husband died, Ruth started to suffer a kidney ailment) so that I will be able to raise my children in the best possible way.

"I also would like to ask for prayer for the leading brothers here, who carry a lot of responsibility in spreading the Word. I thank God for the local believers who help me a lot in caring for the children and raising them; they really encourage me spiritually and help me materially, so it lightens my burden. Pray for my mother who lives with me and helps me to take care of the children.

"I have hope that I will see Mansour, my husband, again in the kingdom of God; I believe that I will see him again. Then he will also see Danny whom he hasn't seen here on Earth."

THE FUTURE

It is likely that by 2050 the Christian church could well number more than two million members. If the current regime remains in power, light restrictions should continue. A change in government, however, could place a stricter Islamic theocracy in control and close the window of opportunity.

PRAYERS FOR THE SUFFERING

1. *The current secular government has been greatly used by God.* Praise God for the government's tolerant attitude toward Christianity, going so far as to permit Bibles to be distributed in public schools. Pray that the church will be able to make use of these many opportunities.

2. *The church has been hurt by the ongoing warfare.* Many Iraqis have died before they could hear the good news of Jesus Christ. Pray for an end to the wars that have lasted for decades and for relief agencies to develop programs to minister to the suffering.

3. *Ministry to the Kurds is particularly dangerous.* Christians among the Kurds have been harassed, threatened, and martyred. Pray for the ongoing safety of these evangelists.

Please Pray for the Persecuted Church in:

ISRAEL

Israel is located in the Middle East, bordering the Mediterranean Sea, between Egypt and Lebanon. The total land area makes it slightly smaller than New Jersey. The terrain consists of desert in the south, low coastal plains, central mountains, and the Jordan Rift Valley.

POPULATION
5.1 million (91% urban)

LAND
Southwestern Asia; 8,019 sq. miles (20,770 sq. km)

LANGUAGES
Hebrew, Arabic

RELIGION
82% Jewish, 14% Muslim

CHRISTIANS
297,000, share growing

PERSECUTION
Isolated, growing

RESTRICTIONS & FREEDOMS
Freedom to worship
Freedom to evangelize

IN THE 21ST CENTURY...
There will be continued opportunities coupled with continued persecution.

Israel's 5.1 million people are mostly Jewish, but a small minority (18 percent) are Arab. One in four is under the age of fifteen.

Israel is one of the oldest nations in the world and the focal point of biblical history. After 1,900 years of exile it regained much of its land in 1948, but has suffered five wars in the past fifty years (all of which it has won, though at great cost). Today it enjoys a certain peace, though the peace process continues to move through considerable debate.

The government is a republic with a legal system based on English common law, British Mandate regulation, and Jewish, Christian, and Muslim legal systems. There is political freedom. The government continues to negotiate for peace but is fractured over the correct approach to take.

The nation's economy is one of the strongest in the Middle East, with a gross national product per capita of U.S.$16,100. The unemployment rate is at 7 percent. Despite these good points, the economy has been stressed by new immigrants and military expenditures. Israel receives significant financial aid from abroad.

Judaism is the official religion, and over three-quarters of the nation belong to one of its branches. Most Palestinian Arabs are Muslims of the Sunni tradition.

CHURCH LIFE

Christians form a small percentage of the nation but are continuing to increase their share of the population. Most Christians are Catholics or Orthodox; Protestants number less than ten thousand. Christians are most numerous among Palestinian Arabs.

PERSECUTION

There is freedom to minister within one's own community, except for Jewish Christians, who are not granted any legal rights. There is freedom to evangelize, though it is frowned upon. The government has pressed for new on evangelism, but so far they have not passed. A significant piece of "anti-missionary" legislation was proposed in the late 1990s but did not pass. Many Jews see Christians as the destroyers of the Jewish nation, either through the Holocaust or through proselytization; many Christians support Israel, seeing its significant role in biblical prophecy, to the exclusion of aid to Palestinian Christians.

The number of Messianic believers in Israel has grown significantly in the last two decades. A Messianic pastor says, "Nowadays there are about sixty Messianic congregations in Israel where Hebrew is spoken. It is still difficult, and sometimes even dangerous, to reach out to Jewish people in Israel. But not so long ago it was almost impossible. Apart from some Messianic believers in the worldly seaside resort Eilat, where no orthodox Jew would ever set foot, no one dared to speak openly about Jesus. But more and more have taken courage and are telling boldly about their Messiah. And the Lord has changed lives in the most peculiar ways."

The pastor recalled meeting Ronit on the beach of Tel Aviv. "He looked like a secular Jew. I told him about Jesus, but he kept saying, 'I don't believe you. You are lying.' He reacted the same when I read Jeremiah 31, verse 31 to him: 'The time is coming,' declares the Lord, 'when I will make a new covenant with the house of Israel and with the house of Judah.' He said, 'Look, I'm from an Orthodox family, I know you have a falsified Bible.' I answered him, 'Now wait a minute. This is the Old Testament. You read from the same book.' But I couldn't convince him. In Hebrew the word for *covenant* is the same as *testament* and I noticed that Ronit was shocked by the idea that God has promised a New Testament in his Bible. So I said to him, 'Go to your home and read what is written in your version of the Scripture. Then come back to me and we'll talk further.'"

Ronit went home and read the verse in Jeremiah, which was, of course, exactly the same. He asked his father, who is a rabbi, about it. "What is meant by this new covenant Jeremiah prophesied about?" His father shrugged his shoulders: "Nothing important. Just something that will happen at the end of the times." Ronit wasn't satisfied by this answer. "The Messianic Jews say that this verse concerns Jesus." His father reacted angrily: "Don't you ever talk to one of them again!"

The next day Ronit came to the pastor and admitted the Bible isn't falsified, but he said, "If Jesus is the Messiah, let Him provide me with a job. I have been jobless for three months." After the pastor prayed with Ronit, the young man's mobile phone rang. It was the man who had fired him three months ago, asking him to come back. In that moment Ronit accepted the Lord Jesus as the Messiah.

Shortly afterward Ronit's father kicked him out of the house because of his conversion. Some fellow believers took care of him. But a couple of days later, the rabbi realized that he had lost his son and that everything should be done to win him back. He offered him his own apartment and sent several people who tried to convince him he had made the wrong decision. Among them were people from Yad Lachim, an Orthodox anti-missionary organization. They also came to the pastor, accusing him of being a Nazi.

The pastor says, "You see, if you lead a Jew to Christ, they perceive that as killing a Jewish soul. Swastikas were daubed on my house, people of my congregation were harassed, and in an Orthodox newspaper they published an article about us that was full of lies. 'They lure children with candy to come in their church and then they baptize them,' the article said. 'Don't ever go to this congregation on So-and-so Street, Tel Aviv.'

"But the Lord used this negative publicity in His own miraculous way. A girl from Jerusalem who had been born and raised in an Orthodox family read this article. She had been curious about the Messianic movement for a long time but never knew how to get more information about it. She took the bus to Tel Aviv and visited us. Now she is a believer, too."

THE FUTURE

The church is increasing its share of the nation slowly, mainly through births to Christian households. (Independent indigenous Jewish Christian churches are the exception; they are adding hundreds of converts to their numbers.) By 2050 it is possible that Christians in Israel could number as much as one quarter of the population.

PRAYERS FOR THE SUFFERING

1. *The church enjoys freedom to minister but must be discreet in evangelism.* Christians may worship, but when they begin to reach out to the Jewish and Muslim communities it must be done in tactful, quiet ways. Pray that new, creative forms of evangelism will be developed.

2. *The Jewish church suffers from much discrimination.* Atheistic Jews are more welcomed in Israel than Messianic Jews. Jewish Christians are denied any legal standing as a religious group, and many have been denied visas or citizenship. Pray that they will continue to be bold in sharing their faith.

3. *The church suffers from misperceptions.* Israelis often view Christians as Zionists or persecutors. Pray that the gospel will be understood as the ultimate fulfillment of the Jewish heritage and for a true movement toward Christ within the nation.

4. *The church suffers from the ongoing warfare.* Attacks, bombings, and wars have all taken a toll on the church. Pray for an end to the warfare and a just peace.

5. *The church suffers from a certain prejudice.* Many Christians worldwide have ignored the Palestinians in the support for the nation of Israel, yet the Palestinian Muslims are just as much in need of salvation. Pray for an increased global interest in meeting the needs of the Palestinians and sharing the gospel with them.

Please Pray for the Persecuted Church in:

JORDAN

POPULATION	**PERSECUTION**
5 million (72% urban)	Isolated, static
LAND	**RESTRICTIONS & FREEDOMS**
Southwestern Asia; 35,135	Freedom to worship
sq. miles (91,000 sq. km)	Freedom to evangelize
LANGUAGE	**IN THE 21ST CENTURY...**
Arabic	There will continue to be
	numerous freedoms for
RELIGION	tactful witness and a signifi-
93% Muslim	cant opportunity for church
	growth.
CHRISTIANS	
270,000, share growing	
rapidly	

Except for a short coastline on the Gulf of Aqaba, Jordan is a landlocked country. The terrain consists of mostly desert plateaus, highland in the west, and the Great Rift Valley that separates the East and West Banks of the Jordan River.

Most of the East Bank is made up of arid desert. The Dead Sea, which Jordan shares with Israel, is the lowest point on the surface of the Earth (more than 400 meters below sea level).

Over 40 percent of Jordan's five million residents are under the age of fifteen. Three-quarters live in cities, and most live to be seventy years old. Jordan is home to a large number of Palestinians; some estimate that as much as half of the population is Palestinian, and many of these are refugees from Israel. There are small numbers of non-Arabs including Circassians, Shishans (Chechens), Armenians, and Kurds.

Jordan was part of the Turkish Empire until 1918, when the country's borders were laid as part of the agreements on Palestine. It was under British control until 1946, when it became an independent state. It has been involved in three Arab wars against Israel, all of which were lost, and the 1990 Gulf War against Iraq had a deep impact due to the influx of refugees and the deterioration of the economy. The enormous Palestinian population pressures Jordan to take a keen interest in the Arab-Israeli peace process.

The economy is poor, with an estimated gross national product of U.S.$1,520 per capita. Unemployment is estimated at 20 percent. The poverty and general deterioration of the economy has caused political turmoil. The constitution grants the king both executive and legislative powers, although from time to time the king has ruled as an absolute monarch. The legislative house is split between the Senate (which is appointed by the king) and the National Assembly (which is elected by the general populace). Jordan's well-liked King Hussein died in 1999, and his son has ascended to the throne.

A solid majority of the country is Muslim, nearly all of whom are Sunnis. There is a small minority of Alawites near the border with Syria.

CHURCH LIFE

The first Christians came to Jordan during the time of the apostles, and their descendants remain in the land today, maintained by the zealous Orthodox clergy. They have long been socially successful and are found in virtually all walks of Jordanian life, particularly among merchants and office workers. Although they have experienced some decline in recent decades, they are presently enjoying a spurt of growth.

PERSECUTION

The constitution establishes Islam as the state religion but guarantees the free exercise of religious belief and prohibits religious discrimination. The sensitive religious and political situation has caused most Christian workers to keep a low profile, but many opportunities remain open. The *Jesus* film, for example, has been seen by more than one half million viewers, resulting in hundreds of converts. There have been some attacks on Christian establishments (such as bookstores) by radicals, but these cases of persecution remain isolated and sporadic.

In Amman, the country's only Protestant seminary, the Jordan Evangelical Theological Seminary (JETS), is having a growing impact on Jordan and surrounding Arab countries despite some opposition. Originally registered as an educational institution in 1995 under the Ministry of Culture, the seminary began its classes in rented facilities. After receiving a large grant in 1998 to buy property and build its own campus, the board of directors finally bought land in 1999 after a nine-month snag in obtaining Intelligence Services (IS) approval for the land purchase. During the delay, three of the seminary's foreign students were detained and forcibly deported by IS officials. All three were former Muslims who had converted to Christianity, had legal residency in Jordan, and were registered officially as JETS students.

At the time of this writing, the seminary was seeking formal accreditation from the Jordanian Council of Higher Education. According to seminary president Dr. Imad Shehadeh, JETS had already experienced "two major miracles" through the initial 1995 registration and the 1999 land-purchase approval. "Now JETS needs one more miracle," Shehadeh said, "and that is accreditation by the Council of Higher Education." Essentially, such approval by the Ministry of Education would constitute a totally new registration, including full recognition of the seminary's treatment of Christian theology as an academic discipline. The anticipated accreditation would give the Protestant seminary permanence as an established university under the Jordanian Ministry of Education. JETS is jointly supported by the Baptist, Christian and Missionary Alliance, Free Evangelical, Assemblies of God, and Nazarene churches established in Jordan.

With a student body averaging more than one hundred full-time students from Jordan and a dozen other countries, the seminary's curriculum includes bachelor's and master's degree programs designed to train Arab church leaders for Christian ministry. Under its current registration, the seminary has been authorized to educate, grant theological degrees recognized abroad (although not formally accredited in Jordan), and give residence visas to its staff, faculty, and foreign students.

Meanwhile, Jordan's evangelical churches were given full permission in early March 2000 for three days of special millennium celebrations for Easter in Amman. The unprecedented event in the 6,000-seat Roman amphitheater in downtown Amman included Christian book exhibitions, multiple *Jesus* film showings, special children's programs, highlights of Jordan's biblical history, and rallies each evening featuring international and Jordanian choirs, musicians, and guest speakers.

THE FUTURE

The church is growing rapidly in numbers but remains a very small portion of the Jordanian population as a whole. Nevertheless, there is an enormous openness, particularly among refugees and intellectuals. It is possible that by 2050 the church could number more than 600,000 believers.

PRAYERS FOR THE SUFFERING

1. *The church enjoys broad freedom.* It is presently using this freedom to share its faith. Pray that the openness will continue under the new king and be enhanced by mass-communication media (such as shortwave radio programs).

2. *The church must continue to be sensitive to the religious climate.* Opportunities for witness demand tactful and discreet response. Pray for the distribution of literature and evangelistic videos through Christian bookstores, as these have been particularly fruitful.

3. *The church suffers from attacks by radicals.* Some ministries have been firebombed and some leaders have been threatened with assassination. Pray that Christian leaders will continue to be bold in sharing their faith and that the government will continue to support Christians against persecution.

Please Pray for the Persecuted Church in:

NORTH KOREA

POPULATION	RESTRICTIONS & FREEDOMS
24.0 million (62% urban)	Conversion can be punished by arrest, imprisonment
LAND	No open evangelism permitted
Eastern Asia; 46,540 sq. miles (120,538 sq. km)	Christian leaders often arrested on contrived charges
LANGUAGE	
Korean	
RELIGION	**IN THE 21ST CENTURY...**
70% nonreligious/atheist, 25% ethnic faiths	The government may launch a new wave of restrictions or may open up to ministry.
CHRISTIANS	
450,000, share growing	
PERSECUTION	
Harsh, growing	

Located in the northern half of the Korean Peninsula, North Korea is made up mostly of hills and mountains separated by deep, narrow valleys. About two-thirds of the countryside is densely forested.

About twenty-four million people live in North Korea. One-third are under the age of fifteen, and nearly two-thirds live in urban areas. Most live to be about fifty years old. North Korea's population is 99 percent Korean; there are small numbers of Chinese but very few minority groups. Because of this, as in South Korea, the gospel could travel very fast while encountering few cultural barriers.

North Korea has been through a long and trying period. Japan occupied the country from 1910 to 1945; it was partitioned between North and South by Russia after World War II. In 1948 Communist leaders gained control, then invaded the South in 1950. The war lasted three years with victory going to the South Koreans while causing significant hardship. The demilitarized zone between the two nations remains one of the most fortified and impenetrable in the world. War nearly broke out again in the late 1990s but was averted by diplomatic efforts. Tensions between the two nations remain high.

Today North Korea is a Communist state ruled by a one-man dictatorship. The country, as a whole, remains closed to the outside world, but economic hardship and widespread famines have caused some openings for those involved in compassionate relief ministries.

North Korea's economy is poor; the average Korean earns just U.S.$900 per year. Nearly half work in agriculture or fisheries. Nearly all are literate and educated, but despite modernization, starvation remains a widespread problem. Observers estimate that some three million North Koreans have died of starvation (although North Korean official estimates are far lower, at 220,000).

About two-thirds of North Koreans profess to be nonreligious. The rest practice such Asian religions as shamanism, Confucianism, or Buddhism. North Korea has been deeply marked by a "personality cult" that has elevated deceased dictator Kim Il Sung to the status of a god. The government uses strict controls to enforce the "Juche" ideology on every citizen, including the worship of Kim Il Sung and his son; all conflicting religions are forbidden.

CHURCH LIFE

Less than 2 percent of the population is Christian, even though the area has a long history of Christianity. Before the war it was a birthplace for revival; Pyongyang was 13 percent Christian and home to nearly half a million believers. After the war many fled south or were martyred. Today there are three churches in the capital, but these are mainly "show" churches for propaganda

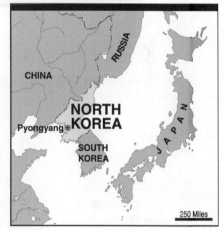

purposes; nearly all believers in North Korea are part of unregistered, underground churches.

PERSECUTION

The persecution of Christians was intense during the period of Japanese occupation, particularly while Japan pressed for the adoption of Shinto as the national religion. Since the rise of the Communist regime, persecution has taken many forms. Christians working for political freedom were first suppressed. The government then attempted to foster Christian support for the regime; failing this, it began a systematic effort to exterminate Christianity. Church buildings were confiscated, leaders imprisoned, and with the failure of the North to win the war against the South, retreating soldiers often massacred Christians in order to prevent their liberation. Since then, the government has required the registration of all churches and their members.

THE FUTURE

Despite the current pressures, the future of the church is bright. The roughly five hundred thousand believers are growing rapidly and are likely to number more than one million by 2050. Many observers of North Korea also think that early in this century many of the current restrictions will be lifted, perhaps with a change in the government. If this happens, we can expect the gospel to pass very quickly through the North Korean population, just as it did in South Korea.

PRAYERS FOR THE SUFFERING

1. *The church feels growing pains.* Praise God for the growth of the church and the ability of Christians to spread the gospel, even in a limited way, in North Korea. Pray that new opportunities for tactful witness will be discovered.

2. *The nation suffers from economic disintegration and widespread famine.* The current disaster is terrible, but God is using it for good: doors are opening to the gospel as the Korean government becomes more and more willing to accept Christian ministries bearing compassionate relief. Pray for this small openness in the government to continue to increase.

3. *The people suffer from an enforced worship of Korea's leadership.* Like King Darius in Daniel's time and the Caesars of the Roman Empire, the government has built a personality cult requiring the worship of the late Kim Il Sung and his son. Pray that the emptiness of this quasi-religion will become apparent and that Koreans will seek the true God.

4. *Ministries to Korea continue to prepare.* Praise God for the large mass of resources being readied to evangelize North Korea. Pray that they will find avenues for discreet ministry today and be prepared to work together in unity when North Korea opens to the outside world.

5. *Extremely creative avenues are required to enter Korea.* Praise God for the many creative means that Koreans have been using to bring the gospel to

North Korea, including floating tracts into Korea on balloons. Pray that these efforts will bear significant fruit.

6. *Korean believers suffer from a shortage of Bibles.* Most believers do not own a Bible and many do not have access to one. Pray that Christian ministries will be able to provide Bibles. Most have to be smuggled into the country; courier teams continue to be needed.

Please Pray for the Persecuted Church in:

KUWAIT

POPULATION 1.9 million (97% urban)	**PERSECUTION** Sporadic, growing
LAND Southwestern Asia; 6,880 sq. miles (17,818 sq. km)	**RESTRICTIONS & FREEDOMS** Freedom to worship Discreet evangelism possible
LANGUAGES Arabic, English	
RELIGION 85% Muslim	**IN THE 21ST CENTURY...** Despite a few highly visible cases here and there, restrictions will be generally light and there will be numerous opportu- nities for discreet witness.
CHRISTIANS 250,000, share growing	

Most people in the West are very familiar with Kuwait, especially after the 1990 Gulf War between the West and Iraq over its invasion of the tiny nation. Kuwait sits in the Middle East on a line between Iraq and Saudi Arabia. It is important for its substantial reserves of oil.

Kuwait is home to nearly 2 million people. About 30 percent are under the age of fifteen, and nearly all live in one of Kuwait's cities; only the hardened nomadic tribes ply the desert sands. Some 47 percent are actually expatriate workers, including Arabs from other surrounding nations and Asians from Pakistan, India, and the Philippines.

Kuwait's government is a "hereditary amirate" with succession through the male descendants of the late Mubarak Al Sabah. A National Assembly represents the populace. Political parties are illegal. The government is dominated by the Al Sabah family, but many other merchant families and Muslim elements have powerful influences.

The government owns nearly 10 percent of the known oil reserves, and its economy is dominated by oil. Nearly everyone works as an employee of the government. Most of the nation's food is imported, although there are some fruit farms and fisheries.

The government provides free compulsory education for all Kuwaitis (and many foreigners); more than three-quarters of the adults are literate. A national health care system provides free medical access to all.

Virtually all Kuwaitis are Sunni Muslims of the Malikite rite. Expatriate Muslims working for the government are mostly Shi'as. In the past the government has spent heavily on promoting Islam (there are several hundred mosques in the land), but with the loss of oil revenues and damage of the Iraq war, this has been curtailed over the past decade.

CHURCH LIFE

The first documented Christian in Kuwait was an American Catholic who entered around 1795. Most of the churches in Kuwait, however, have been started far more recently than that. There are an estimated 250,000 Christians in the nation, a quarter of whom are Catholics and Orthodox. Virtually all Christians are expatriate workers, so that the total number of Christians fluctuates with the total number of foreigners.

The Reverend Amanuel Ghareeb was the first Kuwaiti to enter the full-time Christian ministry, according to the *United Bible Societies' World Report* (April/May 1999). Rev. Ghareeb, who spent twenty-five years in the oil business, received his theological training from a Bible school in Cairo, Egypt, and was recently ordained as pastor of the National Evangelical Church. He is also on the advisory committee of the Book House Company, the center of Bible distribution in Kuwait, and is its legal sponsor. Since it opened last year, the Book House Company has been serving all the Christian churches in the peninsula with the Scriptures in the formats they require.

Reverend Ghareeb, who is married with three children, is one of 250 Kuwaiti Christians. Most of the Christians in Kuwait and in the Gulf are foreigners, either from Western countries such as the United States and Britain, or from Asia, mainly the Philippines and India, working there on contract. Despite the fact that the Christian church has existed in these desert lands since the early journeys of St. Paul, it is unusual to find more than a handful of indigenous Christians, most having embraced Islam for about one and one-half centuries.

PERSECUTION

The 1962 constitution establishes Islam as the religion of the state and utilizes shari'a law as the principle source of legislation; however, it also guarantees religious liberty and the free practice of religion. Compared to many Islamic countries, Kuwait is quite moderate in relating to other religions. Christians residing in Kuwait can meet openly and establish churches, and relations between Muslims and Christians are open and amicable. Media coverage of Christianity and recent conversions have combined with other factors to encourage Kuwaitis to consider the claims of Christ; this has caused increasing tensions.

THE FUTURE

For the time being, it is likely that the church will continue to be a small part of Kuwaiti culture. However, it is equally likely that the air of quiet openness will also continue and discreet witness will be possible.

PRAYERS FOR THE SUFFERING

1. *The church enjoys a climate of relative openness.* Pray that this will continue and that tensions between Muslims and Christians will be eased.

2. *The church enjoys generally friendly relations between Christian and Muslim leaders.* Pray that this will lead to opportunities for interfaith discussion that can be a witness to Muslim clerics.

3. *Overt missionaries are not allowed.* Pray for expatriate "tentmaker" Christians to find discreet opportunities to witness.

Please Pray for the Persecuted Church in:

LAOS

POPULATION
5.3 million (21% urban)

LAND
Southeastern Asia, land-locked; 91,429 sq. miles (236,800 sq. km)

LANGUAGES
Lao, French, English

RELIGION
58% Buddhist, 34% tribal faiths

CHRISTIANS
110,000, share growing

PERSECUTION
Sharp, growing

RESTRICTIONS & FREEDOMS
Limited evangelism
No new church construction
No unapproved religious meetings

IN THE 21ST CENTURY...
There will be continued conflict between Christianity and Buddhism; the government will usually side with Buddhists.

Located in Southeast Asia, Laos is a land of rugged, rusty mountains with a few plains and plateaus. Its northern border is part of the so-called "Golden Triangle," from which flows much of the world's heroin.

Nearly half of Laos' 5.3 million people are under the age of fifteen. Approximately one-fifth live in urban areas, while the majority live in small rural villages. The average life expectancy is just fifty-three years. There are over one hundred ethnic groups, but two-thirds of the population belong to the Lao Loum and 22 percent to the Lao Theung.

Laos is a Communist state with a legal system based on traditional customs, French law, and Socialist practice and lacking in any political freedom. Laos gained its independence from France in 1954 and has been controlled by a Communist regime since 1975. Tens of thousands of people who were sent to "re-education camps" following the Communist victory have now been mostly released by the government.

The average Laotian earns about U.S.$1,100 per year. Of the 1.5 million in the labor force, 80 percent work in agriculture. Laos is the world's third largest producer of opium (from which heroin is manufactured) and has many drug-related problems.

Theravada Buddhism is the official religion of Laos. It is practiced by more than half the population; there are two main Buddhist monastery orders and over nineteen hundred pagodas, as well as more than one hundred schools training about five thousand students. Traditional tribal religions also remain strong; about a third of the population practice them, particularly the non-Lao minorities. A small minority (about 1 percent) adheres to Chinese folk religions.

CHURCH LIFE

The first missionaries to Laos were Catholics in 1630; Protestants began work in 1902. Two-thirds of the country's Christians fled in the early years of Communism, and there were numerous martyrs. Today a little more than 2 percent of the country professes Christianity, though its share of the country is growing rapidly.

PERSECUTION

Although the Laotian constitution contains provisions for religious liberty, the government continues to restrict freedom of religion, force Christians to renounce their faith, imprison believers, and close seminaries. There remain prohibitions on public evangelism, building of churches, and links with foreign organizations. Religious meetings are forbidden without the consent of the Communist authorities, and all religious groups must be approved by an organization under the control of the ruling Communist Lao People's Revolutionary Party (LPRP). Buddhist monks have lobbied for further restrictions on Christian activity, and the government has supported efforts to get Christians to renounce their faith in favor of Buddhism.

Believers in the church in Laos confess that they are going through tougher times and difficulties in the face of surveillance made by authorities. The situation is reported to have worsened in recent months when families of tribal believers who are imprisoned sought refuge in a local church. A total of ten families are said to have been hunted down by the police. Each member of the provincial council was questioned as to whether he or she knew the whereabouts of these families. Those who were questioned admitted to having seen the families and told the police where they were presently staying. All ten families were ordered to return to their communities. At first, the families refused, knowing they would have to face a much tougher ordeal once they arrived back in their villages. But the police insisted they leave. They were so bent on banishing these families that they paid the church a visit every day, until the pressure was too much for the church and eventually the families went back to their villages, despite the threat that was expected to greet them.

An Open Doors source says that each of the families was isolated and was warned against holding fellowships of any kind. "This could be God's way of using these tribal families," states an Open Doors co-worker. "They could be witnesses in the areas where the police have taken them, and they are more in a position to form smaller groups."

THE FUTURE

The church in Laos is growing nearly twice as fast as the population but still is unlikely to have a million members by 2050. The future of the nation is uncertain, but both drugs and Communism are likely to continue to play a significant role for the next generation.

PRAYERS FOR THE SUFFERING

1. *Believers suffer from the impact of the drug trade.* Drugs continue to be a significant problem in the nation. Pray that Christian Laotians are able to resist the temptations associated with the trade, that they will be protected in their stance against the drug trade, and that drug lords will be converted and leave their trade.

2. *Believers suffer from government harassment.* Pray that the government will grant Christians freedom of religion as provided by the constitution and internationally recognized law, for imprisoned believers to be released, and for new churches to be constructed.

3. *Believers have a window of opportunity to evangelize.* Despite the restrictions there are many opportunities for witness. Pray for Christians to boldly evangelize and continue to plant churches. Pray especially for the conversion of government leaders in order to see national change.

4. *Believers suffer from harassment by Buddhists.* Pray for the gospel to be spread among Buddhist monks and to see the spiritual darkness of Buddhism penetrated with the light of the gospel.

5. *Minority groups especially suffer from harassment.* Many Christians among them have been harshly pressured to renounce their faith. Pray that these believers will continue to stand strong and be a witness.

Please Pray for the Persecuted Church in:

LIBYA

POPULATION	**PERSECUTION**
5.7 million (86% urban)	Sharp, static
LAND	**RESTRICTIONS & FREEDOMS**
Northern Africa; 679,362 sq. miles (1,759,540 sq. km)	No evangelism Islamic alms required by law Freedom to worship
LANGUAGE	
Arabic	**IN THE 21ST CENTURY...**
	There will be opportunities
RELIGION	to evangelize discreetly, but
95% Muslim	the growth of the church will likely be met with
CHRISTIANS	increasing opposition.
170,000, share growing	

The size of Alaska and Michigan combined, Libya is the seventeenth largest country in the world. It is mostly desert, with oases on the northwest and coastal plains in the northeast. Yet for all its land, Libya has a small population: just 5.7 million at the turn of the millennium. The numbers are growing quickly (expected to double in just nineteen years); nearly half are less than fifteen years old. The majority live in cities; Tripoli, the capital, is the largest with almost two million inhabitants. Most are Libyan Arabs or Berbers but a sizable minority (21 percent) includes other Middle Eastern nationalities.

The name *Libya* comes from a tribe that lived in the area around 2000 B.C. Through early stages of history the region was inhabited by the Phoenicians, Greeks, and Romans. The fall of the Roman Empire brought the start of Islam's long rule. Gradually the Ottomans united the area and established the Sanusiyah Islamic religious border in 1837. In 1911 Libya was invaded by Italy and occupied, despite fierce resistance. Libya finally gained its independence in 1951 and soon after became a wealthy state with the discovery of its rich oil reserves. Colonel Qaddafi took power and severed ties with the West, establishing Libya as a Socialist state with a single political party. He has financed the spread of Islam as a way of garnering political power in the region. Due to the Libyan government's support for terrorists, relations with the West have continued to worsen and have led to air strikes as well as bans on trade and air travel.

The average Libyan, with an annual income of U.S.$6,500, is poor but better off than his neighbors in Algeria, Chad, or Sudan. Products based on oil make up nearly all the exports; the government controls the oil and most aspects of the economy but often recruits outside help due to a lack of trained workers. The *Qabilah,* or tribe, is the basis of Libya's social structure. Families have an average of five members; schooling is free but two-thirds of adults have no formal education. Medical care is free and made available in well-dispersed patterns, but rural areas still suffer.

Islam spread to Libya from Arabia and Egypt in the late seventh century. Today 95 percent of all Libyans are Muslims (nearly all of the Sunni tradition). Some agitate for the establishment of an Islamic state.

CHURCH LIFE

Christianity has ancient roots in Libya, but its initial failure to evangelize and convert the Berbers, coupled with its weakening in the face of the Donatist schism, rendered it powerless before the armies of Islam in the seventh century. Christianity was all but wiped out, and today there are only a few thousand Libyan believers. Most Christians in Libya are expatriate workers.

PERSECUTION

Although the government of Libya is a secular state, it gives great respect to Islam, conferring upon it an ideological role in society. The government demands respect for Islamic regulations and traditions and requires the submission of all laws to shari'a. Other laws have institutionalized the giving of alms (one of the five ritual obligations of a Muslim believer) by instituting a 2.5 percent tax. At the same time, the government has made some concessions to Christians; it has permitted them to use churches for worship and has, at times, invited foreign missionaries to serve in development roles.

THE FUTURE

The church in Libya continues to grow at a modest pace. By 2050 it will have around 500,000 members, or just under 4 percent of the total population. Persecution will likely continue to be sporadic, with increasing isolated instances of harsh responses to evangelism.

PRAYERS FOR THE SUFFERING

1. *The church enjoys some freedom.* Pray that the church will continue to make effective use of these freedoms to share the Good News of Jesus Christ throughout the nation.

2. *Official missionaries are not permitted.* There are some roles for tentmakers and Christian expatriates. Pray that Christians around the world will be able to learn of these roles and seek to serve Libyans with the love of Christ.

3. *The church endures a government that finances the spread of Islam.* Libya continues to place Islam in a leading role and to contribute to Islamic missions around the world. Pray for the leaders of Libya to come to know Christ.

4. *The church endures calls to establish a theocratic government.* Radicals in Libya have repeatedly called for the establishment of an Islamic state in Libya. So far the government has resisted this. Should Qaddafi lose power, it is uncertain what form of government would succeed him. Pray for the continued maintenance of a secular state and its associated freedoms for Christians.

Please Pray for the Persecuted Church in:

MALAYSIA

POPULATION	**CHRISTIANS**
22 million (54% urban)	1.7 million, share growing
LAND	**PERSECUTION**
Southeastern Asia (includes part of the island of Borneo); 127,320 sq. miles (329,758 sq. km)	Isolated, growing
	RESTRICTIONS & FREEDOMS
	No evangelism
LANGUAGES	**IN THE 21ST CENTURY...**
Malay, Chinese dialects, English, Tamil	The church will continue to grow and the nation will face increasing religious tension, leading to much public discussion and debate.
RELIGION	
55% Muslim, 18% folk-religionist, 7% Hindu, 7% Buddhist	

Malaysia is located in Southeastern Asia, consisting of a peninsula and one-third of the island of Borneo. The land is defined by coastal plains that rise slowly into hills and mountains. Nearly two-thirds of Malaysia is covered with dense forests.

Some twenty-two million people live in Malaysia. One-third are under the age of fifteen. Nearly 60 percent of the residents are Malay while 26 percent are Chinese and 7 percent are Indian. Slightly more than half live in cities, while the rest live in rural villages.

Malaysia has been independent from Great Britain since 1957. In 1963 Sabah and Sarawak joined to form Malaysia, a federation of thirteen states. Recent years have been dominated by the efforts of the politically powerful Malays to extend their influence over the non-Malay, half of the population in educational, economic, and religious life. The growing power of the fundamentalist Muslim political parties has further polarized the nation, with inter-ethnic and inter-religious conflicts.

The government in Malaysia is a constitutional monarchy based on English common law. Malaysia has had its share of wars but now mainly faces internal tensions within ethnic and religious groups. There is some political freedom but it is mostly given to the Muslims.

The economy is growing quickly, measured at U.S.$11,000 per capita. Unemployment is low, estimated at less than 3 percent. Most adults are literate and work in either manufacturing or agriculture. Petroleum is a major export, but Malaysia also exports a variety of other goods, including electronics.

Almost half of the population is Muslim. There are significant minorities of Hindus and Buddhists, and 2 percent of the population hold to traditional animistic faiths. Christianity is the second largest religion in the land.

CHURCH LIFE

Protestants and Catholics number more than half a million members each. Many of the churches are fully under indigenous leadership. Christians have numerous ministries in Malaysia, including hospitals, radio broadcasts, and church planting programs.

PERSECUTION

Malaysia is an Islamic nation and a strong promoter of Islamic solidarity throughout the world. Under Malaysian law it is unlawful for a Muslim to convert to another religion. Anyone caught witnessing to a Muslim can be fined and jailed for a maximum period of two years. Malays comprise nearly 60 percent of the population and form the largest single religious group in the country. The majority of Malays are Muslim and are allowed to receive religious instruction on Islam in schools, but no other religions are permitted this privilege. Christianity, however, is the fastest-growing religion in Malaysia.

THE FUTURE

Nearly all of the denominations and church networks within Malaysia exhibit rapid growth trends. It is probable that by 2050 the church will number more than three million members, increasing its share of the population to more than 10 percent. Persecution will probably increase to sporadic attempts to control and restrict church growth.

PRAYERS FOR THE SUFFERING

1. *The church is enjoying growth*. Praise God for the many new believers, and pray that the church will be able to adequately disciple them and commission many new evangelists.

2. *The church has opportunity to evangelize*. There are many restrictions and Christians must act with discretion, but there also remain chances to share the gospel. Pray that Christians will act with discernment and wisdom.

3. *There are a large number of expatriates from other countries in Malaysia*. Pray that the church will be able to evangelize these workers, who might not be reachable in their homelands.

Please Pray for the Persecuted Church in the:

MALDIVES

POPULATION	**PERSECUTION**
287,000 (27% urban)	Sharp, little change
LAND	**RESTRICTIONS & FREEDOMS**
Indian Ocean islands; 115	No evangelism
sq. miles (298 sq. km)	Muslims may not convert
LANGUAGE	**IN THE 21ST CENTURY...**
Divehi	The large number of
	islands and small number
RELIGION	of Christians will make
99.9% Muslim	evangelism and church
	growth difficult and costly.
CHRISTIANS	
350, share declining	

The Republic of Maldives is a collection of 1,200 islands that lay a thousand miles southwest of India. The islands are home to some 280,000 people, ethnically a mix among Indian, Sinhalese, Arab, and African elements. Nearly half of Maldives' residents are under the age of fifteen; the population is growing rapidly, expected to double in size before 2025. Three-quarters of the population live in rural villages; the largest city, Male, has just 63,000 residents. Nearly all of the adults are literate.

Fishing and tourism dominate the economy; several hundred thousand tourists visit the Maldives each year. The economic condition of the islanders is poor compared to the rest of the world; the average worker earns less than U.S.$1,000 each year.

The Maldives were settled in the twelfth century by Buddhists. In 1314 the leader of the island, a Buddhist named Dharumasantha Rasgefanu, converted to Islam and took the name of Muhammed bin Abdullah. He made the island into a Muslim sultanate, and it was ruled as such until the twentieth century. In 1968 the island was proclaimed a republic.

With very few exceptions, the inhabitants of the island are Muslims of the Sunni tradition. There is a small minority of Buddhists among the Sinhala.

CHURCH LIFE

There are an estimated three hundred and fifty Christians in the Maldives. The church on the islands has historically been tied to the churches in Sri Lanka, particularly the Catholics. Worship services are mainly small groups that meet together privately for informal Bible readings.

PERSECUTION

Islam is the official religion of the Maldives; its legal system based on Islamic law. The rights of individuals are recognized, but they may not contradict Islam. Evangelism is not permitted. Until 1985 there were no known Christians among the Maldivian people, but in recent years small numbers of new converts have been meeting to worship God and study the Bible.

Up to fifty Maldivian Christians were arrested recently for their faith, according to Christian Solidarity Worldwide. The believers were rounded up by the Muslim authorities after a Christian radio program was broadcast in their language. In jail they were pressured to renounce their newfound faith and return to Islam. It is claimed they were forced to take part in Islamic prayers and read the Koran. Christians have been ostracized by their families and neighbors and many have lost their jobs.

The last prisoner to be released was 32-year-old Aneesa Hussein. Before her conversion, she had discussed, debated, and argued about the Christian faith over many months. At first, she could see little difference between Islam and Christianity. But she began to think again when her husband divorced her. Aneesa prayed about her situation, and, as a friend recalled: "Over a number of weeks God touched her husband's heart to care for her. She saw this as an answer from God and wanted to know more about Jesus." Gradually she grew in faith and learned to forgive. Relations with her husband improved.

While in jail, a prison officer threatened to kill her because she was an infidel. Yet Aneesa related that she had a real sense of God's presence in prison and was aware that her brothers and sisters worldwide were standing with her.

The wave of arrests on the islands began after police were given a tip-off by teenagers. One of the informants was Aneesa's own son. Aneesa was placed in solitary confinement and warned she would be kept there until she returned to Islam. She told her husband, "They can keep me in prison for ten years, but I will not turn back to Islam. It has nothing for me."

The arrests came as no surprise to the other Maldivian believers. They had read about persecution in the Scriptures. But they knew that God's power, love, and presence would be with them to help them through. Their faith made a significant impression on other Maldivians. "For the first time they saw their fellow countrymen choosing to put their trust in Jesus, despite sacrifice, suffering, and hostility." The Maldives may appear to be a tourist paradise, but, according to Aneesa's friend, "under the idyllic surface run darker cultural patterns. Forgiveness is rare."

People believe in and despair of hell. In Islam they have little hope of heaven. There is no Cross, Resurrection, or salvation, and little sign that God is interested in or loves individuals. Maldivians are now beginning to recognize that a few individuals with political influence should not have the power to decide what is ultimate truth for all Maldivian citizens.

THE FUTURE

The very small church is not presently growing at a significant rate. With the present restrictions enforced by Islamic traditionalists, it is unlikely that Christianity will make great strides among the Maldives in the near future.

PRAYERS FOR THE SUFFERING

1. *The church is losing converts to Islam.* Pray for a reinvigoration of the church to find new ways to evangelize and plant churches.

2. *The church suffers from a lack of global interest.* Pray for Christians around the world to gain a vision for the Maldives, perhaps to serve as missionaries there. Pray for Christians in Sri Lanka to develop fruitful evangelistic ministries to the islands.

3. *The economy is based on tourism.* Pray for Christians to host prayer journeys and vision-raising trips to the Maldives.

Please Pray for the Persecuted Church in:

MAURITANIA

POPULATION	**PERSECUTION**
2.6 million (53% urban)	Harassment, growing
LAND	**RESTRICTIONS & FREEDOMS**
Western Africa; 397,955 sq. miles (1,030,700 sq. km)	No evangelism
LANGUAGES	Conversion punishable by death
Arabic, Pular, Soninke, Wolof	**IN THE 21ST CENTURY...**
RELIGION	A substantial infusion of outside effort will be required to see church growth, and this may come at the cost of harsh perse-cution.
99% Muslim	
CHRISTIANS	
6,500, share rapidly declining	

Mauritania is located in Northwest Africa, bordering the North Atlantic Ocean, between Senegal and Western Sahara. It also neighbors Algeria and Mali. The total land area exceeds one million square kilometers, which makes it slightly larger than three times the size of New Mexico. The terrain in Mauritania is made up mostly of the barren flat plains of the Sahara, with some hills.

Some 2.6 million people live in Mauritania, half of whom are under the age of fifteen. A little more than one-half live in cities while the balance lives in rural villages. Major ethnic groups include White and Black Maures as well as numerous minorities of African groups (Fula, Soninke, Wolof).

Mauritania had been a French colony for centuries but gained its independence from France in 1960. Since then it has suffered numerous ethnically centered wars. Today it is a republic with a three-tier legal system made up of Islamic courts, special courts, and state security courts.

The people are fairly poor, with an average annual income of U.S.$1,750. Most work in agriculture, and unemployment is very high. The average family has eight members. Only a third of the population is literate, the technological infrastructure is poor, and health services are dismal—all factors contributing to the poverty of the land. Starvation is common.

Islam took control of the region in the tenth century and successfully converted the Berber tribes. Nearly all Mauritanians are Muslims of the Sunni tradition, although many continue to follow tribal traditions as well.

CHURCH LIFE

Christianity came to Mauritania early in the twentieth century, spread by Catholic priests and missionaries. Less than 1 percent of the population is Christian; there are only a few thousand believers in all. Most are Catholics, nearly all of whom are foreigners (primarily French). There are a few Protestants in the capital, but for the most part they have been unable to begin any substantial work in the nation. Most evangelism is aimed toward immigrant workers from Sub-Saharan Africa.

One source reports, "We are making progress in Mauritania although the number of converts is low. A few years ago we had no believers but now we have a few house churches. We live in a strongly Islamic society, so everything we do must be in secret. Our biggest fear is not from the government but that of being discarded by our families with nowhere to go. To be in isolation without the sense of community is one of our biggest concerns. Social control is a big issue here."

PERSECUTION

The constitution establishes Islam as the official religion but guarantees liberty of conscience and religion. In practice, however, evangelism is prohibited and conversion from Islam is punishable by death. There have been numerous martyrs and it is likely there will be many more.

THE FUTURE

The small church in Mauritania lacks the training and resources to be able to effectively evangelize the whole of the nation. The severe restrictions and persecution are more barriers to reaching the nation with the gospel. Without a significant change either in local attitudes or in external help, Mauritania is likely to have only a small outpost of Christianity at the end of this century.

129

PRAYERS FOR THE SUFFERING

1. *Few are interested in the situation of Christians in Mauritania.* Pray for Christian missionaries to begin successful ministries to Mauritanians.

2. *The church endures substantial restrictions on its activity.* Pray for the government to soften its stance and to uphold its guarantee of freedom of religion by permitting individual Muslims to convert to Christianity without threats of death.

3. *Believers suffer from the poverty of the nation.* Pray for Christians to serve Mauritania's poor economy with economic and community development programs that will help to increase good relations between the church and the government.

4. *The church is suffering from a decline in numbers.* Pray for the few Mauritanian Christians to become bold evangelists for their faith and to share their faith with other Mauritanians as they are directed by the Lord.

Please Pray for the Persecuted Church in:

MOROCCO

POPULATION 19.6 million (53% urban)	**PERSECUTION** Sharp, growing
LAND Northwestern Africa; 172,414 sq. miles (446,550 sq. km)	**RESTRICTIONS & FREEDOMS** No evangelism No conversion
LANGUAGES Arabic, Berber dialects, French	**IN THE 21ST CENTURY...** Efforts by the government and organized Islam to suppress Christianity will likely continue to prevent significant church growth.
RELIGION 99% Muslim	
CHRISTIANS 175,000, share declining	

Morocco forms the northwest corner of the African continent, just a few miles from the southern tip of Spain. Half of Morocco's nineteen million people are under the age of fifteen. Less than one-third are literate. Two-thirds are Arabs, and the remaining third is divided between the various Berber tribes and small minorities of Europeans.

The area that makes up modern Morocco was often fought over in ancient tribes by the various world empires. The Arabs invaded Morocco in A.D. 682, and nearly all of the inhabitants of that time quickly accepted Islam, the only exceptions being the Jews. Berbers from Morocco were conscripted and used in the subsequent invasion and occupation of Spain. Thereafter the politics of Morocco remained dominated by Islam until the 1400s, when the Europeans began to invade the area. The Portuguese, Spanish, and French all fought for control; it would eventually be divided mainly between France and Spain.

After World War II, nationalists began agitating for an independent Morocco. France rejected these claims until 1956, when both France and Spain finally recognized the independence of Morocco and it was united into a single country. Sultan Muhammad V assumed the title of king.

Today Morocco is governed by a constitutional monarchy. Its new constitution, adopted in 1996, is somewhat more democratic; the parliament is now elected entirely by popular vote. However, along with the reforms, the king's supremacy remains assured.

Virtually all of Morocco's residents are Muslims. Islam is the state religion, and the overall permeation of Islam into the society has been profound. Moroccan Muslims, with few exceptions, belong to the Sunni tradition. There are about 175,000 Christians and a small minority of Jews and Bahai's, all of which are in steady decline (mostly through persecution or, in the case of the Jews, emigration to Israel).

CHURCH LIFE

Christianity arrived in Morocco in the first century after Christ, and by the end of the second century several bishoprics had been established. Unfortunately, the church suffered terribly in the ensuing years due to Roman perse-

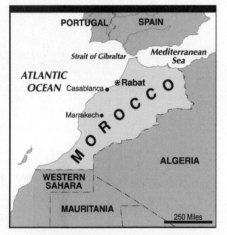

cution, church schisms, and Vandal invasions. Muslim armies put the final end to Christianity's presence in the region. A new missionary effort was begun by the Franciscans in 1220, but evangelism has been suppressed and the church has remained weak. The positive attitude of church leaders toward the independence movement helped improve the general attitude toward Christianity. Nevertheless, the church has declined from nearly half a million believers in the 1950s to 175,000 today. A large majority of these are French and Spanish expatriates and immigrants from such Middle Eastern countries as Syria and Jordan. Indigenous Moroccan believers number less than fifty thousand, and they generally have minimized all outward efforts that might draw undue attention to themselves.

PERSECUTION

Article 6 of the Constitution declares Morocco an Islamic state guaranteeing "freedom of religion" to all. The Penal Code, however, imposes penalties ranging from six months to three years in prison for evangelism—the government is dedicated to the preservation of Islam. While the Moroccan Supreme Court ruled in 1985 that apostasy does not constitute a criminal offense, local police and judiciary have continued to arrest and prosecute Moroccan nationals who have changed their religious affiliation. Christian workers in the area have been arrested and sentenced to prison for evangelism.

A brother shared the following:

"When you look at the indigenous Moroccan church, I have to say that the number of Moroccans who have made a decision for Christ is very limited. Out of a total population of around nineteen million, there are only a few thousand believers. We cannot organize ourselves as a truly open church. We have to meet as house fellowships, and there are a few dozen of these spread over all the country, with larger concentrations found in the cities. It is difficult for us to establish a real working model for the Moroccan church.

"Indigenous leadership is weak and most of our literature comes in unofficially. When it is known that we have left Islam to be a Christian, the pressure to turn back is great. They beat us, imprison us, and even offer us incentives to return to Islam. Believers who come from strict Muslim backgrounds have the most problems. Morocco is more like a police state, where all forms of fundamentalism are unwanted. The king presents himself as a devout Muslim and mainstream Islam is promoted. It has taken a century to get the church this far, so we do not expect fast growth for the church."

THE FUTURE

Although the church today is growing, it is doing so very quietly and very slowly. By 2050, it is possible that the church will double in size, reaching more than 300,000 members, if this growth is supported. However, without a significant change in the current climate (which will probably be accompanied by severe persecution), it is unlikely Christianity will form a significant portion of the country in this century.

PRAYERS FOR THE SUFFERING

1. *Persecution has been steadily increasing for decades.* Pray that the Moroccan government will grant Christians true freedom of religion with freedom to worship and evangelize. Pray for the safety of believers and for a softening of the government's stance.

2. *The church cannot evangelize openly.* Pray that Moroccan Christians will continue to find new, creative ways to spread the gospel and see new believers brought into the church and that their evangelistic efforts will be protected from suppression by the power of the Holy Spirit.

3. *Seekers are subject to intimidation.* Contacts with foreign organizations are illegal and subject to prison sentences. Nevertheless, Moroccans continue to contact Christian radio programs to request study materials. Pray for their safety and for the materials to arrive without being intercepted.

4. *Expatriate workers have been discovered, arrested, and expelled.* Pray for their protection and effectiveness. Many find tactful opportunities for witness. New workers are constantly moving in to join them.

Please Pray for the Persecuted Church in:

MYANMAR

POPULATION
45.6 million (26% urban)

LAND
Southeastern Asia; 261,228 sq. miles (676,577 sq. km)

LANGUAGES
Burmese, indigenous

RELIGION
87% Buddhist, 4% Muslim, 6.3% Christian

CHRISTIANS
2.7 million, share rapidly growing

PERSECUTION
Sporadic, growing

RESTRICTIONS & FREEDOMS
Freedom to worship
Freedom to evangelize

IN THE 21ST CENTURY...
The church will see significant growth and could transform Myanmar into an important Christian base in Asia.

Myanmar (Burma) is known as the "land of pagodas." It is located in Southeastern Asia, bordering the Andaman Sea and the Bay of Bengal, between Bangladesh and Thailand. Its heavily forested land is characterized by central lowlands and is ringed by steep, rugged mountains.

Myanmar has about forty-five million people; one-third are under the age of fifteen. Three-fourths live in rural villages. There are a great many different ethnic groups, the largest of which are the Burmese, the Karen, and the Shan.

The earliest recorded history of Myanmar began in A.D. 107 with the Bagan Dynasty. The first Myanmar Empire was founded in 1044 by King Anawrahtar. During the time of this empire, great multitudes of Buddhist pagodas were constructed. With the invasion of Genghis Khan in 1287, many of these pagodas were destroyed. Between 1287 and 1824, Myanmar was ruled by six separate dynasties; the First and Second Anglo-Burmese Wars were fought in 1824 and 1852 respectively. In 1853, under King Mindon, a massive industrial revolution took place alongside the discovery of oil. In 1885, the third Anglo-Burmese War was won by Britain, who captured Myanmar in its entirety. With the onset of World War II, the Burmese helped the Japanese in an attempt to expel the British colonists; Myanmar gained its independence in 1947 and became a federal union of seven districts and seven minority states. Successive governmental regimes have varied in their relationship with the church. Some have given increasing power to Buddhists while others have been reluctant to involve themselves in religious affairs at all. Popular demand for democracy led to elections in 1990, in which the opposition party won 85 percent of the seats, but the military regime refused to hand over power. After this turn of events, civil unrest broke out; the government quashed the insurgency and arrested, exiled, or killed most of its leaders. The current regime continues to harshly crack down on all insurgents.

The average Burmese worker earns about U.S.$1,000 per year. Most are literate, but many are involved in terrible industries of sin. Burma is the world's largest illicit producer of opium, used to manufacture heroin; there are serious problems of drug use and prostitution. The economy as a whole is mixed between private and state-controlled; the government owns substantial sectors of industry including energy, heavy manufacturing, and the rice trade.

Most of Myanmar's people adhere to Buddhism, which entered Myanmar during the first centuries after Christ. It has been the dominant religion since the ninth century and has had enormous influence over the nation. About 4 percent of the population is Muslim, mainly among the Arakan people of the southwest near the border of Bangladesh. Traditional faiths are practiced by the Montagnard people and influence the actual practice of Buddhism.

CHURCH LIFE

Christianity entered Burma with the Nestorians in the tenth century. Roman Catholics were present in the mid-1500s, and Protestants arrived in 1813. Response to Christianity has varied widely, but Myanmar remains a significant base for Christian ministry in Asia. Some 6 percent of the population in Burma is Christian.

PERSECUTION

There is sporadic religious freedom and sporadic persecution. Some governments in the past have given significant power to Buddhists and restricted the church harshly; others have restricted Christians as an exercise of socialistic atheism, rather than out of concern for the propagation of Buddhism. However, some governments have approved church construction and new resources such as printing presses. Tribal Christians are often persecuted by the government, which sides with the powerful Buddhist lobby and attempts to use Buddhism as a method to control the tribal peoples.

At this time, a war is raging between a military dictatorship and rebel ethnic groups. The policy of "divide and conquer" is the order of the day. Burmese soldiers torment Christians and show favoritism to Buddhists while attacking refugee camps.

On March 11, 1998, just after midnight, seventeen-year-old Sheh Wah Paw and her fifteen-year-old sister, Thweh Ghay Say Paw, prayed quietly. Nearby, soldiers were burning bamboo huts in the border region of Thailand and Burma. Many Karens were without shelter, and Sheh Wah Paw was thanking God for the family's bamboo hut. The thatched family hut was built just a short distance from the Baptist church that they regularly attended. They thought the location was a blessing, but at this moment it was to be a trial.

Kyaw Zwa, the father, had dug a makeshift concrete bunker as a hiding place. Fearing that their home would be destroyed, the girls huddled with their parents in the bunker, hoping for protection. But soon their house was on fire and the heat was so tremendous that the bunker became like an oven. The blaze spread and clothing caught fire. The girls ran screaming from the bunker. Within two weeks both had died from their burns.

One leader was quoted as saying, "This is not a war between the Christians and the Buddhists. It is between the Burmese and the Karen. But they are using religion as a tool to divide people." As in this case, the Baptist church was among the first buildings to be torched, but the Buddhist monastery and the homes surrounding it were untouched.

Kyaw Zwa, saddened by the loss of his daughters, said, "[The Burmese] hate the Karen. But they hate the Christian Karen more." He pondered for some time why the prayers of his daughters had no apparent answer, but now he has peace. "I know that God helped me and that He allowed my two daughters to die. They are gone. But they are free."

THE FUTURE

Myanmar's church is exhibiting rapid growth and could have more than ten million adherents by 2050. Persecution will likely remain sporadic and eventually decline to low levels.

PRAYERS FOR THE SUFFERING

1. *The church has enjoyed rapid growth.* Pray that this growth will continue and that church leaders will develop sound methods for discipling new believers and commissioning them as evangelists.

2. *The church endures attacks by Buddhists, who seek to restrict Christian activity.* Pray that Christians will find ways to effectively respond to these attacks and to earn the respect of government leaders and serve Myanmar.

3. *The church has a substantial impact throughout Asia.* Praise God for the wide scope of ministry directed by works based in Myanmar. Pray that work originating from Myanmar will continue to have a region-influencing impact.

4. *The church and the nation suffer from the impact of drugs.* Intercede against the drug trade that dominates much of Myanmar's economy. Pray that Christians will find workable methods to oppose the drug trade and provide the Burmese people with economic alternatives.

Please Pray for the Persecuted Church in:

NEPAL

POPULATION	**PERSECUTION**
23.9 million (11% urban)	Isolated, growing
LAND	**RESTRICTIONS & FREEDOMS**
Southern Asia, landlocked; 56,827 sq. miles (147,181 sq. km)	Constitutional freedom of religion Freedom to change religion Freedom to worship No evangelism
LANGUAGES	
Nepali, Maithali, Bhojpuri, other indigenous	**IN THE 21ST CENTURY...**
RELIGION	Church growth is a perceived threat to Hinduism; Hindu leaders will call for restrictions on Christianity; radicals will attack Christian workers.
90% Hindu, 7% Buddhist, 3% Muslim	
CHRISTIANS	
150,000, share rapidly growing	

Nepal is a small mountain-ringed nation lying in the Himalayas between China and India.

Most of its nearly twenty-four million citizens live in the hills and the Kathmandu valley; only 11 percent live in urban areas. Kathmandu, the largest city, has one-half million residents. Despite its density and the ruggedness of the land, Nepal is rapidly growing: more than 40 percent of Nepalis are under the age of fifteen, and the population is projected to double before 2025. The people belong mainly to the Nepali and Bihari ethnic groups.

The average Nepali earns less than U.S.$200 annually. The economy is based on subsistence agriculture and has few ties with the outside world. The difficult terrain has led to slow development, but the enchanting nature of Nepal's natural beauty and innate mysticism have drawn thousands of visitors and helped create a thriving industry based on tourism.

Nepal is the world's only Hindu kingdom. Before the 1950s it was extremely isolated, but in 1962 the king assumed direct power in a new governmental system without any political parties. Civil unrest in the 1990s led to sweeping liberalization; Hinduism remains the state religion, but new laws enacted in 1991 granted freedom of religion and worship (although evangelism remains illegal).

Hinduism has given rise to a complex caste system (which was officially outlawed in 1963 but still continues to influence the land). The king of Nepal is thought to be a reincarnation of Vishnu, a Hindu god. There are some other religions: Mahayana Buddhism has a large following, mainly on the borders with Tibet, and many Indian settlers and traders follow Islam.

CHURCH LIFE

Christianity has come to Nepal fairly recently. Indian missions have been working in the country since 1952, but were generally expected to confine their ministry to Indians. The United Mission to Nepal formed in the 1950s and represents hundreds of foreign missionaries and indigenous staff who work together primarily in community development with the approval of the government. Since no foreign missions were permitted to plant churches among Nepalis, Nepali

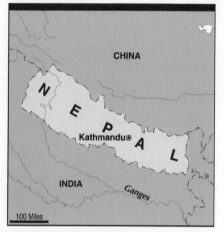

Christians organized the Church of Christ in Nepal in 1966. Today there are about 150,000 Christians, who are rapidly planting new churches.

PERSECUTION

Nepal has been called a country "growing into persecution." The rapid expansion of the church has not escaped the notice of the nation's Hindus, many of whom are calling for new restrictions on church planting and evangelism. So far these tensions have not overly restrained the growth of the church; the most limiting factor has been the lack of trained leadership. This could very well change in the future.

THE FUTURE

Nepal will likely continue to see the church expand for the next decade. As it does, persecution will increase markedly. Already some foreign Christian workers have been expelled, but more severe persecution is possible, including the arrest of Nepali Christians as well as sporadic martyrdoms.

PRAYERS FOR THE SUFFERING

1. *The church is seeing rapid advance.* It has been growing particularly in the outlying areas largely due to signs and wonders. Almost all who have come to Christ have come as a result of a miracle of some sort.

2. *The church endures persecution.* There are two militant Hindu parties that continually harass and persecute Christians: the Shiva Sena and Pashupati Sena, which openly oppose even the presence of Christians in Nepal. Churches have been torn down and believers tortured by these groups.

3. *It is illegal to proselytize.* Stiff penalties are assessed for water baptisms or evangelism. Nepalis generally follow the same religion as their father. Pray for Christians to be bold in the work of the Lord.

4. *The church has had some success in unity.* Pastors have banded together to resist the efforts to suppress their work, but victory has been dependent on the government in power at the time. Pray for Christians to develop appropriate responses to persecution.

Please Pray for the Persecuted Church in:

NIGERIA

Nigeria is located in Western Africa, bordering the Gulf of Guinea, between Benin and Cameroon. The country is made up mostly of lowlands that merge into central hills and plateaus, with mountains in the southeast and plains in the north.

The nation is home to more than 111 million people, making it one of the most populous countries in all of Africa. Nearly half of its citizens are under the age of fifteen. With an average family size of six, the population continues to grow rapidly. Nigeria has numerous ethnic groups, of which the largest are the Hausa, Yoruba, Ibo, and Fulani.

Seeking to dominate the trade along the Niger River and its tributaries, Britain won control over the area that is now Nigeria during the late nineteenth and early twentieth centuries. In 1914 the British created modern Nigeria by forming three distinct regions: the heavily Islamic north, where the Hausa and Fulani people live; the southwest, home of the Yoruba people; and the southeast, where the Ibo and Igbo peoples live.

In the 1930s nationalists demanded autonomy for Nigeria within the British Commonwealth. Many of these leaders were great politicians and had been educated abroad. Nigeria finally gained its independence in the 1960s; Nnamdi Azikiwe, known as the "father of Nigerian independence," had completed his graduate work at the University of Pennsylvania and Lincoln University and played

POPULATION
111.5 million (41% urban)

LAND
Western Africa; 356,669 sq. miles (923,768 sq. km)

LANGUAGES
English, Hausa, Fulani, Yoruba, Ibo, indigenous

RELIGION
49% Christian, 45% Muslim, 6% tribal

CHRISTIANS
54 million, share growing

PERSECUTION
Concentrated in the north, growing

RESTRICTIONS & FREEDOMS
Freedom to worship
Freedom to evangelize

IN THE 21ST CENTURY...
Nigeria will become an important spiritual base and a significant battleground between Islam and Christianity.

a major role in negotiating and installing the independent government. Today Nigeria exists as a federation of more than thirty states. It has been ruled by a succession of Muslim-dominated military governments since 1983, but a controlled transition to civilian, democratic government is now in motion. The legal system is based on a mix of English common law, Islamic law, and tribal law. The country has been torn by wars in the north, sparked by the many coups; there is political freedom but Muslims have significant influence and favor.

The oil-rich economy continues to be troubled by political instability, corruption, and poor macroeconomic management. Nigeria has, unfortunately, failed to make significant progress in diversifying the economy away from over-dependence on the intensive capital oil sector. The average Nigerian earns U.S.$1,300 per year, and over 28 percent of the potential labor force is unem-

ployed. Many lack education; more than half of all adults cannot read or write.

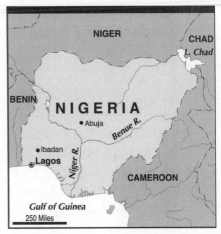

Nearly half of Nigeria is Muslim; 6 percent practice tribal faiths that have been passed down for generations, and about 49 percent are Christian.

CHURCH LIFE

The church numbers more than fifty million members and is growing rapidly. Christianity has penetrated many of the smaller ethnic groups but has yet to make a significant impact on the Hausa and Fulani.

PERSECUTION

While there is freedom to evangelize, evangelists face significant opposition from Muslims, and there have been many martyrs (particularly in the north). Between 1982 and 1996, northern Nigeria faced more than eighteen major conflicts between Christians and Muslims; more than six hundred Christians were killed and two hundred churches were burned.

Nigeria is still living under threat of a religious war. Northern states like Zamfara have declared shari'a law, the Islamic legal code that forbids the sale and drinking of alcohol, the intermingling of men and women in public, and change of religion. Despite the assurances that the controversial law will be applicable to Muslims only, Nigerian Christians, non-Muslims, and others fear persecution and discrimination under the legal regime.

Brother Tikikus was from the Fulani tribe and came from northern Nigeria. He became a Christian in 1972 through the preaching of some Christians. He was one of the strongest believers and witnesses, and through him nine other Fulani men came to know Christ.

However, Tikikus' zealous witnessing and teaching became a threat to others, and he was murdered on May 16, 1999, by another Fulani man—a Muslim fanatic. Although he was prepared to die for his faith, he was not aware that his life was in immediate danger. He was ambushed and beaten with sticks; he died of head injuries, and was found by church members. Fellow Muslims encouraged the murderer to try to make it look like an accident. The accused was caught and taken to the chief. He took his clothes off and ran away naked, pretending to be insane. He was arrested and taken to a psychological hospital, where he was found mentally fit. A Muslim ruler in the area later released him (on the grounds of his insanity), and that was the end of the matter.

Tikikus left behind a wife and six children. The handful of believers that make up the church there will seek to support the family. Brother Tikikus' wife, Li'atu, receives no gratuity from his former employer because he didn't work there long enough. Additionally, she is not educated, so her chances of finding work are slim. She does not own a home and the produce from her small farm is not even enough to meet the needs of her family, let alone sell anything at the market.

Regardless of the hardship, Li'atu is prepared to pay the price for her faith. She said, "If I were not prepared to pay the price for following Christ, I would not have left Islam to become a Christian, neither would I have married a Christian husband." She recalled that the day before Tikikus's death, he had shared with them 1 Peter 3:8–15 and encouraged them to consider their suffering in Christ as the right thing because it is worth it to suffer for Him.

THE FUTURE

The church is presently growing at a moderate pace and could number more than 140 million (over half the nation) by 2050. Along the way there will likely be a sharp increase in tensions between Muslims and Christians, and the nation could become a significant spiritual battleground.

PRAYERS FOR THE SUFFERING

1. *The church has enjoyed rapid advances.* Pray that the north will be permeated with new evangelistic initiatives.

2. *The church has not yet made a significant impact on the large numbers of Hausa and Fulani.* Pray that Christian evangelists will dedicate their lives to bringing the gospel in new, significant ways to these groups, both of whom are part of demographically large populations in Africa.

3. *Workers in the north suffer constant harassment.* It is extremely dangerous to evangelize in the Muslim-dominated north of Nigeria, and many Christians have been killed. Pray for the boldness and courage of evangelists to work in the north, and pray for their safety as well.

4. *The church has the potential to become a strategically important sending base.* Nigeria's large population and economic foundation make it an important African missionary-sending country. Nigerian Christians serve as evangelists throughout Africa, particularly in the north. Pray that Nigerian churches will continue to send missionaries across the whole continent.

5. *The church enjoys some interest from abroad, but not as much as it should receive.* Pray that the global body of Christ will find new and meaningful ways to partner with the Nigerian church to see their nation, continent, and the world as a whole, reached with the gospel.

Please Pray for the Persecuted Church in:

OMAN

Located just below the United Arab Emirates on the border of Saudi Arabia, Oman is a mountainous land on the strategic tip of the Musandarn Peninsula, dominating the entrance to the Persian Gulf.

Oman has a population of some 2.5 million; half are Omani Arabs and 15 percent are Balochs. Because of its limited access to water and the

POPULATION 2.5 million (78% urban)	**PERSECUTION** Isolated
LAND Southwestern Asia; 82,030 sq. miles (212,457 sq. km)	**RESTRICTIONS & FREEDOMS** Expatriates have freedom to worship No freedom to change religion
LANGUAGES Arabic, English, Baluchi, Urdu, Indian dialects	Freedom to evangelize expatriates No freedom to evangelize Muslims
RELIGION 90% Muslim, 9% Christian, 1% Hindu	Muslims may not attend services
CHRISTIANS 240,000, share rapidly growing	**IN THE 21ST CENTURY...** There will be little immediate personal danger despite ongoing restrictions.

high mountains cutting the interior off from the Gulf, Oman has one of the most distinctive cultures in the Persian Gulf states.

Britain exercised a brief protectorate over the island, although Oman has maintained its independence, in principle, since 1650. It was a federal monarchy until 1970 and has been an absolute monarchy since then. No political parties are permitted, although there is considerable personal freedom. Oman is the only state in the Persian Gulf where the ruler is referred to as the sultan.

A substantial minority of the population, and more than 70 percent of its work force, is made up of foreign expatriates. Because of this, the religious climate of Oman is more relaxed than in many other Muslim states. Socially, Oman faces many problems. It is laboring to provide adequate housing and utilities (particularly water), increase food production, and discourage urban migration. Oman's economy is dominated by oil, but the government has labored to wisely invest its wealth in development programs and the diversification of agriculture and industry.

Islam is the official religion of the state. Most Muslims in Oman are Ibadi Kharijites. There is a small minority who practice Hinduism, mainly Indians, Pakistanis, and Sri Lankans, who serve as expatriate workers in the oil fields.

CHURCH LIFE

Although Christian communities were present in Arabia as early as the first century after Christ, they almost certainly were not established in Oman. The triumph of Islam in the seventh century led to the total eradication of Christians from the region. The first missionaries were Catholic priests from Yemen in 1841. Zwemer pioneered Protestant missions in Oman in 1889. Today the Christian community in Oman is almost entirely expatriate; indigenous Omani believers are estimated at around twenty. There are no established churches or networks, and individual Omanis have little fellowship with each other due to secrecy.

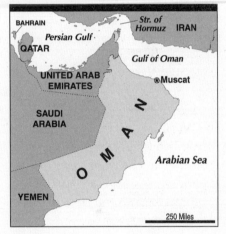

PERSECUTION

As in the United Arab Emirates, many religious freedoms are granted to expatriate workers. Church services are held for several denominations in multiple languages. Further, there are no restrictions on evangelism among expatriates, and this effort has led to a steady flow of Asian converts. Unfortunately, proselytization of Muslims is strictly forbidden. Omanis may not attend services and do not have the freedom to change their religion.

THE FUTURE

Although there will likely be continued freedom for expatriate Christians, it will probably continue at the current price: evangelism of Omanis must be done secretly. It is unlikely that Omani believers will number more than one or two hundred by 2050 without some significant change.

PRAYERS FOR THE SUFFERING

1. *The church enjoys limited freedom.* Thank God for the substantial presence of Christians within the expatriate work force. Pray that they will find opportunities for discreet witness.

2. *The nation has benefited from the government's wise use of its funds.* Pray that Christian community development organizations will be able to serve the government with excellence and integrity.

3. *The church is free to evangelize expatriates.* Pray that this freedom will be wisely used to reach out to the many workers who come from other nations in the Middle East and Asia.

4. *Many Christians remain secret believers.* Pray for their protection and for wisdom to uncover tactful opportunities to share their faith.

Please Pray for the Persecuted Church in:

PAKISTAN

POPULATION 156.4 million (35% urban)	**PERSECUTION** Harassment, growing
LAND Southern Asia; 339,732 sq. miles (879,902 sq. km)	**RESTRICTIONS & FREEDOMS** Blasphemy law prevents Muslims from converting Separate electorates for religious minorities No evangelism
LANGUAGES English, Urdu, Punjabi, Sindhi, Pashto	
RELIGION 95% Muslim	**IN THE 21ST CENTURY...** Christians will be increas- ingly marginalized even as
CHRISTIANS 3.8 million, share growing	they grow ever more quickly; concern over their growth could spark sharp incidents of persecution.

Pakistan occupies a strategic location in southern Asia, between Afghanistan, Iran, and India. The land can be divided into three major geographic areas: the northern highlands, the Indus River Plain, and the Balochistan Plateau. The climate is generally arid, with hot summers and cold winters.

The country has 156 million residents, a figure expected to double by 2050. The population is comprised of several ethnic groups, the major ones being the Punjabi, the Sindhi, the Pashto, and the Baloch. Although Urdu is the official language, English is in general use.

Pakistan and India share one of the oldest recorded histories in the world. One of the first religions to impact Pakistan was Buddhism, which developed some five hundred years before Christ. Ashoka's empire spread Buddhism throughout the region. The second religion was Islam, which conquered the Sindh region in A.D. 711; by the 1200s the Delhi sultanate had been declared. A century later it was destroyed by Tamerlane, who conquered much of Asia. His empire lasted for nearly a century before the rise of the Mughal Empire; it, in turn, would last some two centuries before the coming of the British. The European phase of Pakistan's history (while it was still part of India) was marked by several major conflicts. In 1947 India was granted its independence and partitioned into India and Pakistan (split into West and East areas). The next twenty years saw ongoing violence, political instability, and war between Pakistan and India. In the mid-1980s Pakistan moved ever closer to Islam.

Today the government of Pakistan has taken various forms (parliamentary, military, and presidential), as the system evolves toward more stability. The current government is a parliamentary system with a bicameral legislature; civil laws must be reviewed by the Federal Shari'a Court to decide if the law is acceptable in the context of Islam. Pakistan's principle ties are with the West, the Persian Gulf states, and China. Its relations with India remain tense.

The economy is marked by widespread poverty; the average Pakistani makes less than U.S.$500 yearly. About a third of adults are literate. Substandard housing, inadequate water supplies, and poor sanitation systems all contribute to disease and high mortality rates; only one-third of the population has access to safe

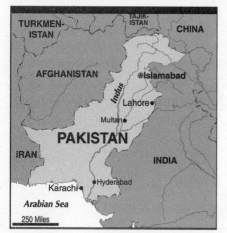

drinking water. Only one in four children attends school, and three-quarters of the population are illiterate. One of Pakistan's less well-known products is heroin, yet it provides much of the Western world's supply.

More than 95 percent of Pakistan's residents are Muslims. Islam was declared the state religion of Pakistan in 1956, and Pakistan is a base of Muslim missionary activity worldwide. About 1 percent are Hindus.

CHURCH LIFE

Christianity was brought to Pakistan by Nestorian missionaries in the eighth century. Jesuits picked up missionary work in the 1500s, but neither the Nestorians nor the Jesuits succeeded in establishing a lasting work. Today, as a result of a wide variety of missions, Pakistan has a small minority of Christians, most of whom are Punjabis. The church continues to add thousands of members each year, mainly through births to Christian families. Most Christians are either members of independent indigenous Pakistani churches or of the Roman Catholic tradition. The Christian community is, on the whole, fragmented and fearful; there may be thousands of secret believers, but few Muslim converts have openly identified themselves for fear of retribution.

PERSECUTION

Pakistan's "blasphemy law" has received significant attention in Western media over the past decade. Though no Pakistani Christian has yet been executed after being convicted under it, more than a dozen have been charged and forced to live in fear and wretched conditions in prison, in hiding, or in exile. However, many Christian workers in Pakistan say the blasphemy law is not the real problem; instead, the root lies with the country's system of separate electorates for religious minorities. This system has been labeled "religious apartheid" and "the main root cause of persecution of Christians and other religious minorities." It gives religious minorities a small, fixed number of seats in the National Assembly; 207 out of 217 seats are reserved exclusively for Muslims, with the remaining ten divided among Christians, the Hindus, the Parsees, and the Ahmadiyyas. It is thus very difficult for religious minorities to influence laws or policies, and no politician has sufficient incentive to take up the case of Christians falsely accused of blasphemy.

One of the highest-profile Christian prisoners in Pakistan has been Ayub Masih, who was convicted of alleged blasphemy in April 1998. His death sentence was the apparent catalyst for the suicide of Bishop John Joseph of Faisalabad, who shot himself outside the Sahiwal courthouse where Masih had been convicted and sentenced.

Despite mounting pressure and protests from church leaders and human rights activists, little has changed for Masih, or Christians as a whole. In February 1999, Masih survived a second attempt on his life while in prison—he was attacked by four prisoners armed with knives. This took place at the celebration for the end of the Muslim festival Ramadan, where prisoners were allowed a little more freedom of movement in the prison. A timely intervention by prison guards prevented more serious injuries. At an earlier court hearing, a bullet missed its mark as an attempt was made to assassinate him.

"I never considered that being a Christian was 'unlucky,'" Masih told Compass Direct news service. "Rather, I consider myself 'lucky' because I am suffering for Christ's name." He stressed that everything that has happened to him has strengthened his Christian faith.

Masih was jailed in October 1996, after a young Muslim neighbor in the Punjabi village of Arifwala accused him of blasphemy against the prophet Muhammad. Local Christians maintain that the case was concocted to win a land dispute against the Masih family. No evidence was produced in court apart from the sole claimant's accusation, but still the lower court ruled Masih guilty.

The fact that all Christians accused of blasphemy in Pakistan have eventually been freed, albeit after terms in prison, encourages Masih. But he is also aware that most have been forced to seek asylum abroad, fleeing ongoing murder attempts by Muslim extremists—a situation his mother and family dread.

THE FUTURE

The Christian church continues to grow rapidly and could number more than 14 million by 2050. Persecution will likely increase to markedly sharp levels. The border with India could become a flashpoint, with dire consequences for the Christians living there, particularly those in the disputed Kashmir region.

PRAYERS FOR THE SUFFERING

1. *The church in Pakistan is largely Punjabi.* Pray for the Christians in Pakistan to develop a broad cross-cultural church that embraces all of the people in the nation.

2. *The church endures a strong governmental bias against it.* Pray for Pakistan's authorities to soften their stance and permit non-Muslim faiths to have a broader representation in the government.

3. *Christian leaders are often harassed and threatened.* Pray for Christian leaders to continue to boldly evangelize, make disciples, and train new leaders in order to plant the church throughout the land.

Please Pray for the Persecuted Church in:

PERU

POPULATION	**PERSECUTION**
25.6 million (71% urban)	Isolated, growing
LAND	**RESTRICTIONS & FREEDOMS**
Western South America;	Constitutional freedom of
496,225 sq. miles	religion
(1,285,216 sq. km)	Freedom to change religion
	Freedom to worship
LANGUAGES	Freedom to evangelize
Quechua, Spanish, Aymara	
	IN THE 21ST CENTURY...
RELIGION	Christian workers will
97% Christian	be opposed by drug
	producers, guerrillas, and,
CHRISTIANS	on occasion, government
25 million, share rapidly	soldiers.
growing	

Peru is a moderately-sized country in the western half of Latin America. It is characterized by three zones: a dry coastal plain in the west (where most of the cities and industry are located), a high plateau in the Andes mountains (marked by agriculture), and the upper Amazon jungles in the east.

Peru's population of 25 million is growing slowly; a little more than one-third are under the age of fifteen, and the population is not expected to double until well after 2050. The people are split evenly between Amerindian people and Spanish-speaking Mestizos and Whites. Nearly three-quarters live in urban areas; Lima, the capital and largest city, has more than five million residents.

Most Peruvians are literate and educated, but poor and unemployed. Peru has been termed one of the riskiest nations on Earth for business thanks to climate changes, global economic recession, disease epidemics, and guerrilla warfare. The government has successfully dealt with hyperinflation, but unemployment remains staggeringly high, estimated at over 50 percent of the work force.

Peru gained its independence from Spain in 1824 and since has had a long history of dictatorships and military regimes. An attempt at democratic government in the 1980s failed miserably, leaders being unable to deal with the terrible economic problems; meanwhile, terrorist movements were responsible for twelve years of war that cost 26,000 lives and $10 billion in damage. President Alberto

Fujimori suspended the constitution in 1992 and began personally running the government in an attempt to bring change. While terrorism has been brought under control, peace remains elusive. In 2000, Fujimori won an unprecedented third five-year term in a disputed election.

Although the largest part of the country is Christian, some 2 percent follow traditional tribal faiths. Additionally, a third of Roman Catholics are estimated to be "Christopagans," meaning that they still practice much of their traditional superstitions while adhering to a thin veneer of Christianity.

CHURCH LIFE

Explorers brought Catholic priests to Peru in 1536. Catholicism was made the official state religion in 1845. More than 97 percent of the country professes

Christianity, of which 89 percent are Catholic. Christianity is in a marked crisis but has great potential for the near future. Most of its clergy are foreigners, and its members argue unceasingly over liberation theology. Discipleship has been hampered by a lack of trained priests and pastors, so Christopaganism has run rampant. At the same time, national difficulties have sparked tremendous interest in Christianity and growth in evangelical churches, and Evangelicals have become a significant force for social change. Likewise, the charismatic movement has made a deep impact, but, unfortunately, many of those involved have splintered away from existing traditions and denominations to form small, independent bodies with little power or influence.

PERSECUTION

When the Roman Catholic tradition was declared the state religion, foreigners were granted permission to hold Protestant worship services, but Peruvians were not permitted to attend. Religious freedom was guaranteed in the 1978 constitution, but Catholics continue to hold tremendous influence. Meanwhile, persecution of Christians by terrorists and soldiers became severe in the 1980s; an estimated eight hundred Christian leaders have been martyred, and many congregations have been massacred. Christian evangelists working in areas of conflict, or drug production, have been particularly at risk.

Among the thousands of victims of the violent years of civil war in Peru (between the country's military and the Shining Path guerrillas), the Saune-Quicana family has paid a high price for the cause of the gospel.

Justiniano Quicana, the family's patriarch, became a Christian when he heard the gospel. As a result, the entire family accepted Jesus Christ as their Savior and came fully under His lordship.

One of Justiniano's grandsons, Romulo Saune, whose life story was told in the book *One Bright Shining Path*, also became consumed with passion for God. His short life was but an example of God's mercy. After he translated the Bible into his native Quechua of Ayacucho, he traveled to very dangerous places to deliver it to his beloved Quechua people. Donna, his widow, and their four children, Romi, Cusi, Qori, and Tawa, now carry on the work of the gospel in Chosica, Peru.

Romulo, his brother Ruben, and two of their cousins, were killed in an ambush by Shining Path guerrillas in September of 1992 as they traveled to Ayacucho to visit the gravesite of their grandfather, Justiniano, who had been brutally assassinated by the subversives not too long before.

Josue, Romulo's brother, lived in the United States at the time of the killing. His heart immediately was filled with revenge, and he traveled to Peru for the sole purpose of avenging his brothers' murder after the burials. However, as he stood up to speak at the funeral services, the Lord turned his heart completely around, and his wrath was replaced with God's forgiveness and a vision to serve his people. Josue is now living in Peru with his Native-American wife, Missy, and their two children; he's fully committed to traveling the Andes to bring the gospel to his people, the Quechuas, in their own language. He's already the target of death threats and has been warned not to go into certain areas. But Romulo's words still ring loud and clear in Josue's ears: "We are immortal until the Lord calls us home!"

As Romulo preached the gospel in an Ayacucho village in 1979, all its residents, all members of the Saune clan, accepted Jesus as their Lord. One of them, Juan, who attended the recent Agape Training seminar in Vinchos, said that only his and his father's families survived the Shining Path's rage. Between 1979 and 1988, about forty of his close relatives were murdered.

Thus, the suffering of this entire family has been great. Of all the victims, some have been casualties of the violent years of war, but most died because of their love and commitment to their Lord. They believe with all their hearts that their mission in life is to bring as many Quechuas to Jesus as they can. Enrique Saune, Romulo's aging father, expressed it well when he was asked when he would retire from his treks from village to village preaching the gospel and baptizing the new believers: "If I don't do it, who else will?"

THE FUTURE

The church continues to grow at a pace equal to the population. Most Peruvian Christians will likely be Catholics, but Protestants could make significant gains. The sting of persecution will continue as well.

PRAYERS FOR THE SUFFERING

1. *The church enjoys a majority position in the nation.* Pray that leaders will devise successful discipleship and training programs to combat nominalism and Christopaganism.

2. *The drug trade dominates the land, and the church feels its impact.* Pray that Christians will develop appropriate responses to the drug trade, including the evangelization and conversion of its leadership.

3. *The church has suffered in the midst of national tensions.* Pray that Christians will be a force for peace and reconciliation, in seeing the costly insurgency brought to an end. Pray for the conversion of terrorists, especially among their leadership.

4. *Believers suffer due to the economic hardships.* Pray that Christian ministries will be able to bring economic development programs to help the struggling nation.

THE PHILIPPINES

POPULATION	**PERSECUTION**
75.9 million (55% urban)	Isolated, growing
LAND	**RESTRICTIONS & FREEDOMS**
Southeastern Asian islands;	Constitutional freedom of
115,831 sq. miles	religion
(300,000 sq. km)	Freedom to worship
	Freedom to evangelize
LANGUAGES	Freedom to change religion
English, Filipino, Tagalog	
	IN THE 21ST CENTURY...
RELIGION	Christianity will continue to
90% Christian, 8% Muslim	dominate the nation
	although it will face grow-
CHRISTIANS	ing challenges from Islam.
66 million, share rapidly	
growing	

The nation of the Philippines is different from most of the countries of the 10/40 Window (which extends from West Africa to East Asia, from ten degrees north to forty degrees north of the equator), in that it is dominated by Christianity. Located in southeastern Asia, the Philippines consist of an archipelago between the Philippine Sea and the South China Sea, east of Vietnam. The islands are made up mostly of mountains with coastlands of varying size. Nearly half of the land is forested.

With more than seventy-five million people, the nation is the seventh most populous in the region and has one of the highest population densities. More than one-third are under the age of fifteen, and it is estimated the population will double in size by 2025. Although more than half live in cities, some 45 percent live in often hard-to-reach rural areas. The capital, Manila, has nearly ten million people in its metropolitan area. Unfortunately, many Filipino cities are dominated by urban slums; some live in the trash dumps on what they can scrounge. More than 90 percent of the population is Malay, but a small minority comes from China and the West.

Most Filipinos are literate, and the nation has slowly modernized itself. Yet although the economy has been gradually improving, it is still poor; the average Filipino earns less than U.S.$5,000 per year. A large number of products are manufactured in the Philippines for export abroad, but most people work in agriculture.

Islam was introduced in the Philippines in 1380 by Malay immigrants. Magellan's expedition brought the first Catholic priest to the Philippines in 1521; Spain annexed the lands and it remained a Spanish colony until 1898. The Muslims were not completely conquered until 1876 and were never fully part of Philippine political life; they strongly resisted Christianization. The Philippines were annexed by the United States in 1898, at which time Protestant missionaries entered the land.

Most Muslims were, and are, concentrated in the relatively underdeveloped southern areas of Mindanao, the Sulu archipelago, and Palawan. In the 1930s overcrowding caused northerners to move into Muslim areas looking for

land to settle. Because many Muslims lacked written claim to their lands, many of them lost their property to the settlers, most of whom were Christians. By 1970, the bitterness of Muslims led to armed revolt against the Christian colonists and the government, and civil war spread throughout the Muslim-dominated districts. Conflict and tension has continued to current time, costing more than 100,000 lives and contributing to political instability and opposition to the gospel. A peace agreement was signed in April 1996, but tensions between Muslims and Christians remains high.

Islam claims about 8 percent of the population. Most Muslims are part of the Sunni tradition; they are usually referred to as *Moros* (the Spanish word for Moor), but they do not like the term because of its negative connotation.

CHURCH LIFE

Christians in the Philippines are predominantly Catholic; less than 10 percent are Protestants. Although the constitution of the Philippines officially provides for separation of church and state, the Philippines are the only majority-Christian nation in Asia and so this provision has been interpreted loosely.

Catholics have tremendous influence in the nation and the government. The Protestant churches have seen marked growth since 1974. Although there are widespread problems with spiritism among Catholics, a new emphasis on personal study of Scripture and the charismatic renewal have touched hundreds of thousands in the Catholic parishes. The Philippines is a substantial base for ministry throughout Asia; the Far East Broadcasting Company (FEBC), for example, airs over 2,200 hours of programming per year from the Philippines, and several literature distribution agencies have printing presses and warehouses there that serve much of Asia. Furthermore, Filipinos have served as missionaries throughout the Middle East, most notably in hard areas such as Saudi Arabia; many have been martyred in their chosen lands of service.

PERSECUTION

The church has complete freedom to evangelize in the Philippines and is supported by the government. Opposition to the gospel continues to come from individual Muslims in the south. Radical Muslims have attacked Christian targets in the past as part of their war against the government and continue to be openly hostile to Christians to this day.

THE FUTURE

It is highly doubtful that Christianity will decline from its position of importance in the near future. The current revival is likely to grow and expand, touching both the Catholic and Protestant traditions. The Christian church has substantial resources and will probably become a powerful base for reaching Muslims throughout Asia and worldwide.

PRAYERS FOR THE SUFFERING

1. *The church needs to be united.* Intertraditional hostilities, particularly between Catholics and Protestants, have prevented the spread of revival and Christianity.

2. *More work needs to be done among the southern Muslims.* Pray for Christian workers evangelizing the south; many live with constant threats and some have been attacked and killed. Pray for the conversion of influential Muslim leaders and for ministries of reconciliation between Christians and Muslims.

3. *Praise God for the missionary vision of the Filipino church.* Many take menial jobs in Middle Eastern countries in order to serve as witnesses. Some have been arrested and expelled, or tortured and executed. Pray for their safety and effectiveness.

Please Pray for the Persecuted Church in:

QATAR

POPULATION	**PERSECUTION**
600,000 (92% urban)	Sharp, rapidly increasing
LAND	**RESTRICTIONS & FREEDOMS**
Southwestern Asia; 4,412	Freedom of worship
sq. miles (11,427 sq. km)	No evangelism
	Muslims may not convert
LANGUAGES	
Arabic, English	**IN THE 21ST CENTURY...**
	Attempts to maintain the
RELIGION	good will of the govern-
93% Muslim	ment may increasingly
	come at the cost of ministry
CHRISTIANS	opportunities.
50,000, share growing	
rapidly	

Qatar is an independent state on a small island jutting into the Persian Gulf off the eastern tip of Saudi Arabia. The terrain is rocky and mostly barren with an extremely hot, arid climate. The island has a population of 600,000, including a large number of expatriate workers who come to work in Qatar from many other states. As a result of the migrants, Qatar has a disproportionately large number of men: two-thirds of the populace is male. A quarter of the residents are under the age of fifteen; the population is growing slowly, expected to double by 2050. Most of the residents are Arabs, but there are some Asian minorities. With few exceptions, the citizens live in urban areas; the largest city is Doha, with more than 340,000 residents.

Qatar has been settled for as long as history records. The first known inhabitants were Canaanites. Islam conquered the area in the seventh century, and Qatar became part, in turn, of the various Muslim empires. Iranians once held influence, but Saudi Arabia took control in the eighteenth century, followed by the Ottoman Turks in the nineteenth century. In 1916 Qatar became a British protectorate. It was granted independence in 1971. During the twentieth century it stayed close to Saudi Arabia and participated in the Gulf War against Iraq in 1991, winning several notable battles.

Qatar is a monarchy based on shari'a law. There is no legislative body, but the constitution guarantees basic rights to all citizens. Banking and oil production dominate the economy, and oil accounts for three-fourths of all exports. Unemployment is very low, but the average worker earns only about U.S.$11,000. However, Qatar's citizens benefit from the largesse of its oil; revenues are used to develop the nation. The government has provided a new road network, hospitals, desalination plants, and a welfare plan that includes free medical care and education.

Some 93 percent of Qatar's residents are Muslims. Islam in Qatar is dominated by the Sunni tradition, primarily Wahhabis, although there are a minority of Shi'as.

CHURCH LIFE

Christianity reached the area in the early centuries of the church and had

grown to considerable size before being virtually eradicated by Islam in the seventh century. Catholics first established the modern church in the 1840s. Estimates of the size of the church range from 30,000 to 60,000. Christians form a substantial portion of Qatar's populace, perhaps as much as 10 percent—but most are expatriates working with the oil companies. There are perhaps a few thousand secret believers.

PERSECUTION

Qatar's constitution declares Islam the official religion of the state and bases law on Islam but guarantees democratic rights. This dichotomy is reflected in the society: although any attempt at evangelism is prohibited, Christian expatriates are free to organize and publicize their worship services, and clergy can enter and travel in the country without restriction.

In late 1999, an exclusive *Gulf Times* report announced a bombshell that is still reverberating across the Arab Gulf: "The way is now clear for establishing the first Christian church in Qatar."

Italian Ambassador Ignazio Di Pace said, "The establishment of a Catholic Church in Qatar has been approved in principle." Calling the decision "yet another sign of Qatar opening up to new vistas of freedom and religion tolerance," the *Gulf*

Times said only the technical and financial details remained to be worked out.

Reportedly, a plot of land is expected to be allotted for use as a Christian church compound in the capital city of Doha. The property would be divided by common agreement among the various Christian communities to construct individual church facilities.

Along with Saudi Arabia, the guardian of Islam's holiest cities of Mecca and Medina, Qatar prohibits the public practice of any religion except the strict Wahhabi interpretation of Islam. However, the government has for several years quietly allowed the Christian communities of Catholic, Orthodox, Anglican, and other Protestant denominations to meet informally for private church worship services, hinged on prior notification to local authorities.

By contrast, all the other Arab states on the peninsula—Kuwait, Bahrain, Oman, the United Arab Emirates, even Yemen—have allowed expatriate Christian congregations to build churches and meet for public worship on designated compounds. Ambassador Di Pace, who was posted to Qatar four years ago, said that the idea of building a church at that time was "unthinkable."

While the emir reportedly supports the liberalized stance on church buildings, government officials are said to be sensitive toward potential opposition from more conservative elements of the Qatari population.

"The Gulf is shaping up to becoming a real testing ground for whether Islam can live with diversity in its midst," a Western church leader, who was born and raised on the Arabian peninsula, told *Compass* recently. "So far as the struggle between moderate Muslims and hard-liners is concerned, the governments must walk a thin line to take any new steps."

THE FUTURE

Qatar's Christian population continues to grow at a modest pace. By 2050, given present trends, it could more than double in size. It is probable that modest restrictions will continue.

PRAYERS FOR THE SUFFERING

1. *The church in Qatar is enjoying growth.* Pray that the new converts will develop a zeal both for home evangelism and for cross-cultural missions to the other nations of the Middle East. Pray for the continued development of effective church planting and discipleship systems to train the new converts.

2. *The church in Qatar is largely expatriate.* Pray for these foreign workers to find ways to quietly share their faith and plant churches.

3. *The church endures only modest restrictions.* Praise God for the limited freedoms provided in Qatar. Pray that the church will continue to have good relations with the government.

Please Pray for the Persecuted Church in:

RUSSIA

POPULATION 147 million (76% urban)	**CHRISTIANS** 84 million, share growing rapidly
LAND Eastern Europe and Northern Asia; 6,592,849 sq. miles (17,075,400 sq. km)	**PERSECUTION** Isolated, growing
	RESTRICTIONS & FREEDOMS Moderate restrictions
LANGUAGES Russian, Tatar, Ukrainian	**IN THE 21ST CENTURY...** Intratraditional persecution could limit the growth of Protestant and Catholic churches.
RELIGION 57% Christian, 30% nonreligious, 7% Muslim	

Russia is the largest nation on the planet, with a total land area of seventeen million square kilometers, nearly twice the size of the United States. It is divided into two spheres by the Ural Mountains: European Russia to the west and Asian Russia to the east. The terrain consists of broad plains with low hills west of the Urals, vast coniferous forest and tundra in Siberia, and uplands and mountains along the south border regions.

Russia's 147 million people are, for the most part, located west of the Urals, concentrated in the cities. Three-quarters of them live in urban areas and 18 percent are under the age of fifteen. For a variety of reasons, the population is in decline; the chief cause seems to be that families have a deteriorating economic situation, making them less able to care for their children. Russians make up the majority of the population, but there are significant minorities of Tatars, Ukrainians, Chuvash, Bashkir, Belorussian, and Moldavian.

Russian workers suffer from a lower middle-class income level. Although Russia's potential wealth is enormous, Communism has devastated the country and shattered the economy. The gross national product per capita stands at just U.S.$2,600, but Russia has plenty of resources: most of the workers are literate, education systems are good, and the nation has an abundance of natural resources.

The present government is a federation based on civil law. There is political freedom, and political parties are permitted. Russia has known autocracy, or tyranny, since it became a country in the eighth century. The Communist revolution enabled Russia to dominate the USSR from 1922 until its final collapse in 1990 when a multiparty democracy was established.

For some seventy years the Communist Party attempted to eliminate all religious affiliation from their nation in the name of eradicating superstition. With the demise of the Party, religion has once again exploded across Russia, as many secret believers have become public confessors and evangelizing forces have saturated the land. About half the population professes some tradition of Christianity. One-third continue to declare themselves nonreligious or atheist, and some 7 percent are Muslim (mainly concentrated on the border with Central Asia).

CHURCH LIFE

The first Christians in Russia were likely Armenians; according to church tradi-

tion, they were converted by the apostle Thaddeus a few days after Pentecost. Today 84 million Russians profess Christianity, although as many as 20 percent do not practice their faith (and this number is growing annually, with estimates that it may reach as high as 50 percent by 2050). A huge majority is part of the Orthodox Church; some 1.5 million each belong to the Protestant and Catholic traditions. However, both Catholics and Protestants are growing at a pace well exceeding that of the Orthodox Church.

PERSECUTION

The church in Russia has experienced one of the most severe and sustained persecutions in recent history, with martyrs numbered in the millions and much of the church's infrastructure destroyed. Today it is still threatened with new persecution, as the government and Orthodox Church react to the wild and unorganized influx of new ministries over the past decade, and the government itself goes through significant stages of turmoil. There continues to be a limited window of opportunity for a significant church movement, the likes of which the world has seldom seen. How long the window will remain open is uncertain, and what the future of Russia will be is equally unpredictable. Peace and religious freedom are especially at risk in the republics of Chechnya, Dagestan, Tarterstan, and Ingushetia.

Anya Hrykin is a thirteen-year-old Baptist girl who spent three months in the hands of Chechen rebels in the city of Groszny in Chechnya, Russia.

In October 1999, Anya escaped from Chechnya and made it to a safe house in southern Russia. Only days later she returned in search of her mother. She never found her. Instead she was caught by a group of Chechen rebels. She was tortured and raped at the hands of her Muslim kidnappers before escaping to neighboring North Ossetia in December 1999.

Anya's captors forced the frail, underfed young girl to recite the Muslim creed and convert to Islam. After hospitalization, she is now back in a safe house near Krasnodar with other members of the Grozny Baptist Church.

Some months before, the rebels beheaded the pastor of the Grozny Baptist Church and his assistant.

THE FUTURE

By the middle of the next century the church in Russia will likely have about the same numbers it does today—perhaps more than 60 percent by 2050—but the makeup of the church will likely be far different. Protestants and Catholics will both have achieved significant shares, and while the Orthodox Church will still remain the dominant player, it will have declined somewhat in total numbers.

PRAYERS FOR THE SUFFERING

1. *The church enjoys enormous freedoms.* Although new laws have served to levy restrictions on the church, Christians still have a tremendous opportunity to share their faith. Pray that the churches will use this opportunity wisely.

2. *The church suffers from a tremendous rift between Orthodox, Protestant, and Catholic arms.* Pray that a ministry of reconciliation and mutual cooperation will develop.

3. *Believers suffer from the poverty of the nation.* Travel, evangelism, and church planting can be difficult for the local pastors. Additionally, evangelistic resources and Bibles are still lacking. Pray that the church around the world will continue to help equip the Russian church for evangelism.

4. *Some republics need special prayer:* Chechnya, Dagestan, Tarterstan, and Ingushetia. All are cases of severe suffering due to local religious conflicts, civil wars, and wars for independence. Pray that the church will be able to serve the peoples of these four provinces with healing, reconciliation, and compassionate aid.

Please Pray for the Persecuted Church in:

SAUDI ARABIA

POPULATION
21.6 million (84% urban)

LAND
Southwestern Asia; 830,000 sq. miles (2,149,690 sq. km)

LANGUAGE
Arabic

RELIGION
99% Muslim

CHRISTIANS
750,000, share static

PERSECUTION
Severe, growing steadily

RESTRICTIONS & FREEDOMS
Conversion punishable by death
Evangelism punishable by arrest, occasional execution
Worship punishable by arrest, imprisonment, deportation

IN THE 21ST CENTURY...
Saudi Arabia will no doubt continue to be the most oppressive of all nations, ferociously guarding the home of Islam and treating severely potential threats to its supremacy.

Saudi Arabia is found at the heart of the Middle East, bordering seven countries and surrounded by the Red Sea, the Indian Ocean, and the Persian Gulf. Much of its land is desert, with the heat and dry air broken up by the rare oasis. The nation's twenty-one million people reside mainly in the major cities: Riyadh (the capital), Jeddah (a major port), Mecca (the heart of Islam, to which all Muslims in the world are required to make a pilgrimage at least once in their life), Medina (another holy city and cultural center), and Ad Dammam.

Saudi Arabia is thought to be the original home of such biblical peoples as the Canaanites and Amorites. Several ancient kingdoms had power in the land before the time of Christ; Alexander the Great had planned to conquer Arabia but died before he could. The first momentous event to mark the land was the birth of Muhammad in A.D. 570. Through his life, Islam was founded in Saudi Arabia in the 600s, and, from that time to this, the historical and political battles have been restricted to various branches of Islam struggling for control.

The second major event occurred centuries later, in 1938. At that time, Saudi Arabia's culture and economy were little different from the time of Muhammad. The people practiced Islam, and camels and tents dotted the deserts. In that year, however, the first petroleum deposit was discovered and the kingdom began an extensive modernization program. Since then, Saudi Arabia has tried to walk a precarious line between contacts with the world and isolation to keep the purity of their faith. Today, Saudi Arabia remains a kingdom governed by a monarchy based on shari'a (Islamic law). In March 1992, a series of royal decrees established a bill of rights, the first such in the land. There is no legislature; the king and his ministers issue laws.

Islam is practiced by 99 percent of the population. Most are Sunnis, though there are minorities of other sects. Saudi Arabia is the heart of Islam and home to the holiest of Islamic holy sites; nearly one million pilgrims come every year. Saudi Arabia is the headquarters for some of the most important international Islamic organizations, notably the Muslim World League, responsible for spreading Islam worldwide through missions, financial support, and broadcasting.

CHURCH LIFE

According to tradition, the apostle Barnabas first brought the gospel to Arabia; before the coming of Islam, there was a large Christian population who even aided Muhammad during his time of exile. When Islam gained control in the seventh century, all Christians were expelled. No missions have been allowed since. Today's believers are almost all foreign expatriates who live and work on military bases or for oil companies. There are only a handful of secret Saudi believers, all of whom live under constant fear of discovery, arrest, and execution. They view potential new converts not with excitement, but with fear and suspicion. This hinders the growth of the church.

PERSECUTION

Saudi Arabia is a monarchy firmly committed to the maintenance of Islam throughout the kingdom and abroad. The king is the spiritual leader (imam) of all Muslims worldwide, holds all power in Saudi Arabia, and is the recognized guardian of the holy places. The government supports the Sunni majority, and the practice of Islam is encouraged by financial reward and enforced by surveillance, arbitrary detention, travel restrictions, and political and economic discrimination against non-Sunnis. The king maintains a personal militia charged with maintaining the public practice of Islam. Private home fellowships for expatriate Christians are prohibited but usually tolerated; evangelism is not. Public worship by any non-Muslim is a criminal offense; any attempt at evangelism is subject to criminal prosecution. Christian evangelists face different penalties depending on their nationality. Those who come from Western allies (such as the United States) will typically be quietly expelled from the country. Those who come from poorer Asian nations (such as Filipinos) have been imprisoned, tortured, and, on occasion, executed (usually on trumped-up charges). The holy city of Mecca is kept completely off-limits to non-Muslims; trespassers may be killed. Further, Christians are at risk from radicals who may attempt to assassinate leaders and from informants who attempt to penetrate the churches. The government offers a bounty of a year's salary—a tempting prize for many—for anyone who reports a home fellowship.

Donnie Lama is one of those Filipino Christians who has been imprisoned and tortured in Saudi Arabia. It started as a case of mistaken identity. Donnie was in the wrong place at the wrong time. But looking back on that fateful day, he is certain that he was serving God's purpose. Donnie, a Filipino contract worker, returned to Riyadh on October 5, 1995, to resume work for an airline company. Three days before his return, a Filipino hospital worker had been killed in Riyadh. The killer was at large and the police began to track him down. An apartment mate of Donnie knew the boss of the murdered man (a fact Donnie was made aware of five days later).

On the night of October 10, police tried unsuccessfully to break into his apartment, but the next day they gained entry. Donnie was arrested and taken in for questioning. The only thing in the apartment of interest was his photo album. His Bible and Christian books had already been taken to a friend's house as a result of the attempted break-in. Donnie was now in the hands of the *mutawa*, the Saudi's dreaded religious police. In spite of being beaten and tortured, the police could not link him to the crime in question. The only thing they had against him was a photograph taken in 1984 showing Donnie officiating at a Communion service for a group of Filipino Christians. He was accused of being a preacher for fifteen years. After spending the night in an underground isolation cell, he was released.

One week later it all began again: handcuffs, pain, brutality, and harassment. The charge now was that of being a "priest" for fifteen years. After a further week of torture, his body swollen and black-and-blue from bruising, Donnie unwittingly put his thumbprint to a document, which ultimately sealed his fate. The so-called admission resulted in a prison sentence. In prison, he found himself ministering to other prisoners, especially those who had lost all hope. After more than a year in prison he was twice called back to court to ask if he had become a Muslim. The second time, on admission that he was still a Christian, he was sentenced to seventy lashes, duly carried out.

Donnie was encouraged by letters sent to him during this time from Christians all over the world. A month before his release he was sent back to the police station where he was first arrested. There he was told that he would be released if his employer provided him with a plane ticket to the Philippines. During what seemed a long delay, Donnie continued his work, and just one day before his final release he was able to lead a suicidal prisoner to Christ. Then, on March 28, 1997, Donnie boarded Saudi flight 864 bound for Manila. It was the Saturday before Easter, and he celebrated his own personal victory over death. Today he has his own mission: he is working to help imprisoned Filipinos and their families as the battle continues.

THE FUTURE

The number of believers is in flux; growth is generally due to expatriate Christians moving into Saudi to work. Saudi secret believers are basically static: they are adding to their numbers but not enough to increase their share of the population. By 2050 they will likely be a very small part of Saudi culture, while the population, as a whole, will have added another fourteen million Muslims. Saudi Arabia regularly and casually violates the human rights of its citizens and expatriate workers, denying them the fundamental religious liberties guaranteed by United Nations conventions. With the rigorous enforcement of its religious policies, it is unlikely the Christian population will grow to become a significant portion of Saudi Arabia's citizenry any time in this century.

PRAYERS FOR THE SUFFERING

1. *The church suffers from poor relations with Islam.* Before the coming of Islam, Saudi Arabia had a large Christian population who came to the aid of Muhammad during his exile. When Islam gained control some 1,300 years ago, Christians were expelled. Today Islam is the official state religion, and all other religions are prohibited. Pray for a return to good rela-

tions between Christianity and Islam that will permit Christian workers to enter the country.

2. *Expatriate workers are unable to worship.* Foreign Christians who live and work in Saudi Arabia (in oil companies or on military bases) are not permitted to gather for worship. However, there are many underground, unofficial meetings that are usually ignored by the government. Pray that these small groups will continue to be tolerated and will become an effective base of witness and fellowship.

3. *Muslim converts face the harshest punishments.* A Muslim who converts to another religion is considered an apostate and may be punished by death. The kingdom maintains a secret religious police force committed to the maintenance of traditional Islam. Muslims who consider converting to Christianity face severe consequences—the least of which is the potential for being completely cut off from their family, friends, society, and place of work. Pray for courage for new converts who must endure this for the sake of the gospel.

4. *The church cannot evangelize.* No Christian evangelism is permitted. Christian literature is banned, and non-Muslim visitors are not permitted in the Islamic holy city of Mecca on penalty of death.

5. *Asian evangelists often face the ultimate consequence of their evangelism.* Filipinos have been especially successful in witnessing. They have come to Saudi Arabia as menial laborers (cooks, maids, and others) and have been able to successfully evangelize their employers. Many have paid the ultimate price. Pray for their continued success.

Please Pray for the Persecuted Church in:

SOMALIA

POPULATION
7.2 million (26% urban)

LAND
Eastern Africa; 246,201 sq. miles (637,657 sq. km)

LANGUAGES
Arabic, Somali, English, Italian

RELIGION
99% Muslim

CHRISTIANS
100,000, share rapidly declining

PERSECUTION
Severe, growing steadily

RESTRICTIONS & FREEDOMS
Conversion can be punishable by arrest, imprisonment, death
Evangelism possible but limited
Christian leaders often threatened by fundamentalists

IN THE 21ST CENTURY...
Warlords and anarchy will continue to oppose Christianity, placing significant barriers against evangelism.

Somalia is the easternmost country on the African continent. Along with Ethiopia and Kenya, it forms a semi-arid tip called the Horn of Africa. The landscape leads downward from the northern Ogo and Migiurtinia Mountains into deserts and savannahs to a subtropical region in the south.

Some 7.2 million people are citizens of Somalia. Of these, more than a million have fled the current anarchy and become refugees in other lands. By 1993 some 250,000 had died as a result of famine and war. About three-quarters of the population belong to one of four clans: the Dir, the Daarwood, the Hawiye, or the Isxaaq. Another 20 percent belong to various southern groups that are looked down upon. A small minority belongs to various Bantu peoples. Three-fourths live in rural communities; nearly half are under the age of fifteen. Less than a quarter of the adults are literate.

Somalis are among the poorest of the poor in the world. The average individual earns U.S.$110 annually. After years of warfare, the economy has been shattered; it is, for the most part, controlled by warlords who deal in drugs, arms, and food aid. Most people get by as subsistence farmers, or cattle herders, and are dependent on humanitarian aid programs.

Somalia became a single formal country in 1960 when the various portions were granted independence by the British and Italians. Somalia has clashed since the beginning with Ethiopia and was funded in large part by cold war economics, receiving subsidies first from the Soviet Union and then from the United States. Conflict, both within and without, has devastated the country and its citizens. A bloody civil war in 1991 unseated the government but left the nation in the shambles of anarchy. The United Nations intervened in 1992 in order to provide food aid to those in need. While chaos and clan fighting continue in most of Somalia, some orderly government has been established in the northern part.

Islam is the official religion of Somalia. With few exceptions, Somalis are Muslims of the Sunni tradition. There are some Hindus among the expatriate Indians working in Somalia.

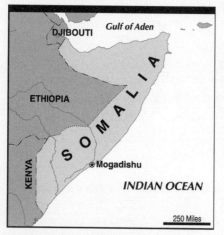

CHURCH LIFE

Christian missionaries began work in Somalia in 1881. They won a few hundred converts before they were forced out in 1974. By 1995 there were more than 100,000 believers in Somalia, but the vast majority of these were refugees from Ethiopia's wars. There are only a few hundred Somali believers, all of whom live under harsh persecution.

PERSECUTION

In 1972 the government nationalized all church property; with the loss of their facilities, most Christian workers left the country. Muslims blame Christian relief organizations for spreading the gospel, and the resulting media attention has led to public attacks on Christianity in the newspapers. Additionally, Muslim political parties have issued reports detailing Christian evangelistic programs and warning Somalis in the strongest terms to stay away from them.

It was in Canada that Muhammad Hussein Ahmed (Haji) heard the gospel in the early 1980s and became a believer. The Somali native was receiving advanced training after graduating from the Lafole University outside the Somali capital of Mogadishu. He returned from Canada and was a professor at Lafole Teachers Training Institute until the civil war. From 1993 he was employed as education coordinator for a nongovernmental organization.

A learned and intellectual person, Haji was working to provide new text-books for the schools that were running in Somalia under very difficult cir-cumstances. He started to feel insecure during late 1994, when Muslim fundamentalists were on the offensive; by then they had already killed five Chris-tians in the area. Haji reported that Muslims had approached him and asked him why he did not go to the mosque. He tried to find all kinds of excuses, but they continued to challenge him. They knew he confessed to be a Chris-tian, but they wanted to test him.

During the last part of 1995 Haji received death threats and considered leav-ing Mogadishu. A few months later, during Ramadan 1996 (January/February) he was very open about his Christian faith. During meals he blessed the food with prayers everyone could hear. A Christian brother reports that Haji believed he was going to be the next to be killed. One morning as Haji and his young son were walking toward the office; a car came up beside him. Some men jumped out, forced Haji into the car, and drove away, leaving his son screaming.

Fellow believers became worried when he did not turn up at the office dur-ing the morning hours. They knew of the threats, but nobody talked about it openly out of fear. The next morning a body was found in the ruins of a nearby house. It was Haji. He had been shot in the neck.

THE FUTURE

Although there are a large number of Christians in Somalia, nearly all of these are Orthodox refugees from Ethiopia who have very little influence on Somali society. There are less than a few thousand indigenous Somali believers. With every sector of society pressed against them, the future of the Christian church in the nation is bleak. Even demographic growth is nil since most Somali believers are unmarried men. Except for the Orthodox Church, all of the Somali churches have declined drastically over the past few decades. This decline does not appear to be reversing, and without a dramatic change, Somali Christianity may be all but eliminated early this century.

PRAYERS FOR THE SUFFERING

1. *The people of Somalia suffer from anarchy.* Warlords, all of whom deal harshly and violently with any perceived threat, presently rule the nation. Each con-trols a specific area and all war with one another constantly. The people of

Somalia are caught in between. Pray for an end to the anarchy and the establishment of a stable government.

2. *Somali believers suffer from constant persecution.* To convert to Christianity is to invite death at the hands of radicals. All live under considerably harsh persecution and fear for the safety of their families and themselves. Many struggle with whether to remain secret or to openly declare themselves and share their faith. Pray for wisdom and protection.

3. *Christian aid groups suffer from attacks by fundamentalist Muslims.* Christian aid groups can offer considerable help to Somalia for the improvement of quality of life. But many operate in Somalia under significant risk: their workers have been threatened and killed, their convoys have been attacked, and their equipment has been confiscated. Pray for improved relations between Christian ministries and those in power.

4. *Christian evangelistic broadcasts suffer from negative portrayals in the press.* Radio and television programs, along with literature follow-up, have seen some fruit. They have come under attack by Somali media as a result. Pray for their continued effectiveness.

5. *The church has been all but extinguished.* Pray for its replanting. With just a few hundred believers a completely new beginning is needed. It may require totally new methods to be successful. Pray for courage and wisdom on the part of Somali church leaders.

Please Pray for the Persecuted Church in:

SRI LANKA

POPULATION
19 million (22% urban)

LAND
Southern Asian island; 24,962 sq. miles (64,652 sq. km)

LANGUAGES
English, Sinhala, Tamil

RELIGION
69% Buddhist, 15.5% Hindu, 7.5% Christian; 7.6% Muslim

CHRISTIANS
1.4 million, share declining

PERSECUTION
Isolated, static

RESTRICTIONS & FREEDOMS
Freedom to evangelize

IN THE 21ST CENTURY...
With growth and outreach will come increasingly sharp attacks from Buddhists and Hindus.

Sri Lanka is a pear-shaped island about thirty kilometers off the coast of India. Mountains dominate the south, some of which are destinations for interfaith pilgrimages. The northern coastal belt falls into plains that end in the mountains. A large portion of the island is forested.

One-quarter of Sri Lanka's nineteen million people are under the age of fifteen. Most live in rural settlements; only 22 percent live in urban areas. Three-quarters of the population are Sinhalese, while Tamils make up 18 percent and Moors, 7 percent.

After nearly five hundred years of being a colonial possession of the Portuguese, Dutch, and British, Sri Lanka gained its independence as a parliamentary democracy in 1948. Attempts to "Sinhalize" national life in the 1950s resulted in ethnic unrest and attempts to create an independent Tamil state in the northeast; all-out civil war erupted in 1983, and tensions have continued ever since.

The government is a republic with a strong executive branch based on a complicated mix of English common law. Freedom of thought, conscience, and worship were established by the 1978 constitution.

The nation is poor largely due to damage from the ongoing civil war, which has crippled the economy; the average worker earns less than U.S.$500 yearly. Tourism at one point was a substantial industry, but this has declined markedly with the civil unrest.

Sri Lanka is a Buddhist nation; almost 70 percent of the population follow Buddhism. Nearly all Sinhalas are Buddhists. Hindus have the next largest bloc, with roughly 16 percent of the population; 7.6 percent are Muslim, and 7.5 percent are Christian.

CHURCH LIFE

Tradition claims that the apostle Thomas first evangelized the island of Sri Lanka. As early as the 500s, visitors to Sri Lanka reported numerous churches and converts. The Portuguese arrived in 1505 and introduced Catholic Christianity; the Dutch, in the 1600s, introduced Reformed Christianity; and in the 1800s, the British brought Anglican Christianity. Today, Catholics claim the largest share (6 percent), while new, independent, Sri Lankan churches claim the next largest bloc,

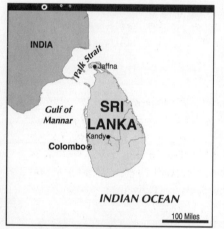

approximately 1.3 percent of the population. The church has been losing considerable numbers of converts back to Buddhism but has been making significant changes in order to reach out to non-Christians.

PERSECUTION

New growth in the church has stirred reaction from the Buddhist and Hindu communities. There has been substantial anti-Christian propaganda in the media, accompanied by accusations against the churches, pleas for new restrictions, and a number of instances of church burnings. Missionary work is restricted and visas are hard to obtain. Work in rural areas is limited, due to restrictions and a lack of workers; many areas have no witness whatsoever.

Some areas of the deep south of Sri Lanka have been particularly hostile to the gospel. Despite the dangers, Lalani Jayasinghe, a remarkable woman of God, has given her life as a "living sacrifice" to serve the Sri Lankans. Lalani married her husband, Lionel, a pastor, in 1986. They worked together through many difficulties to identify with, and minister to, the people. Their work was admired, and the people loved them. Many saw the genuineness of their lifestyle and were drawn to accept the Lord they preached. But they faced great opposition from other religious leaders.

"I am not making people change religions; I tell them that God can change their lives because He did just that for me," said Pastor Lionel.

On March 25, 1988, Lalani and her husband and two fellow church workers were in their home when they heard a knock on the door. One of the workers opened the door and found two men standing there, asking for the pastor. Lalani's husband stepped forward and identified himself. Without saying a word, one of the men pulled out a gun and shot Lionel through the mouth. Clutching his mouth, he ran back into their bedroom where Lalani and the baby were. He fell upon the bed in a kneeling position. One of the men followed him and stabbed him several times, while the other men pumped more bullets into his body. The men fled on foot. None of the neighbors helped; they were understandably terrified.

Lalani managed to get her husband to the hospital, but he was pronounced dead on arrival. Returning home to her blood-spattered bedroom, she was faced afresh with the horrible experience that snatched her beloved husband from her. However, she felt a sense of destiny, that this was not the end but a beginning.

The funeral for Lionel was very tense, and the air was filled with uncertainty about what would happen next. On the grave of her husband was placed a concrete slab with a cross on it. It was the only cross to be found in any cemetery in their area, which stretches for about fifty miles, among a population of about half a million people. But this cross also became a symbol of the living Christ who would express himself through this widow of a martyr, whose blood was shed in Sri Lanka to become the seed-plot of revival.

The leaders of the church were concerned about Lalani's future and tried to comfort her. A pastor offered to move her to a safer area, but Lalani refused, saying, "Every time I see the bloodstains from my husband's body, I am encouraged to stay and continue the vision for which he sacrificed his life."

Twice Lalani received threats that she would suffer a death like her husband's, but she remained undaunted. She continued to bring up her son in the ways of God and remain where her ministry was, and is. She was given many offers to leave her hostile environment and minister in other areas, but she refused.

Lalani's commitment has changed the environment. She and her fellow workers have reached out to all the surrounding areas and have established seven churches that minister to over 1,200 believers.

Her ministry involves hard physical work. She has to walk miles to reach her people—as there is no transportation—and often she spends the night and walks back the next day. This difficulty has given Lalani the opportunity to disciple her people and to influence them to do ministry by her own example.

Lalani still faces opposition from some villagers, but she continues to be bold and tenacious in proclaiming the gospel. She presently serves as a minister in the Assemblies of God/Sri Lanka. Her example has given courage to many who have had to go through persecution. She has also been able to visit the war-torn area of the north of Sri Lanka, and has witnessed to and comforted many that have lost family members to the war.

THE FUTURE

Although the church is adding numbers through births to Christian homes, it is losing enough in defections to Buddhism that its share of the population is in decline. However, the current growth is a reversal of earlier declines, and it seems to be picking up additional speed. There has been a renewed surge in spiritual life, particularly among evangelicals. By 2050, the church may broach some two million members.

PRAYERS FOR THE SUFFERING

1. *The church enjoys limited freedom.* With growth has come reaction, and the limits of the current window of opportunity are already being tested. Pray that the church will work effectively and efficiently to share the gospel boldly.

2. *The church suffers from nominalism.* When it was originally planted, the church generally adopted Western modes and failed to completely contextualize itself within the Sri Lankan culture. As a result, it failed to effectively evangelize and suffered losses to Buddhism. Pray for churches to contextualize the gospel and for a return to biblical theology and holiness.

3. *The church suffers from continuous conflict.* More than 25,000 have died, and over 1.4 million have been displaced, or been made refugees, as a result of the war. Pray for peace in the nation and for the church to become an effective minister of healing and reconciliation.

Please Pray for the Persecuted Church in:

SUDAN

POPULATION	**PERSECUTION**
29.4 million (32% urban)	Severe, growing steadily
LAND	**RESTRICTIONS & FREEDOMS**
Eastern Africa; 967,500 sq. miles (2,505,813 sq. km)	Conversion can be punished by arrest, imprisonment, death
LANGUAGES	Evangelism possible but limited
Arabic, Nubian and other indigenous, English	Christian leaders often arrested on contrived charges
RELIGION	
70% Muslim, 20% Christian, 10% tribal	**IN THE 21ST CENTURY...** Warfare and its subsequent social disruption will continue to pose formidable barriers to church growth.
CHRISTIANS	
5.5 million, share rapidly growing	

Sudan is the largest country in Africa, located in the northeastern corner of the continent. It is made up of two distinct regions: northern Sudan is mostly desert, while southern Sudan is made up of plains, grasslands, and tropical bush.

Christian missionaries converted the whole area of Sudan around the sixth century, but the thirteenth and fourteenth centuries saw the Christian kingdoms conquered by Muslim forces. Conflicts between Egypt, Sudan, Ethiopia, and Britain gave rise to the Anglo-Egyptian Alliance in the late 1800s, which stood through two World Wars and into the 1950s, when growing nationalism led to Sudan's total independence. Afterward, it disintegrated rapidly into civil war and has since suffered nearly twenty years of conflict, followed by a decade of tense peace. Conflict resumed when, in the early 1990s, Islamic fundamentalists took power in the government and pushed through new rules declaring shari'a law throughout the land. Southern Christians protested, and when they were ignored, they took up arms.

The Sudanese people are among the poorest of the poor, and Christians are the worst off. Nearly 2.4 million Sudanese are threatened by famine caused by the current civil war. Soldiers have displaced citizens, stolen cattle, and burned villages; arable land has remained untilled due to the constant flux of refugees. Despite massive relief efforts by the United Nations World Food Program (such as the delivery of 15,000 tons of food in August 1998), starving refugees see little relief. Part of this is caused by the continuous halting of aid by the government in Khartoum in retaliation for rebel attacks, and part is due to the fact that many rebel troops have skimmed food aid for their own soldiers.

Islam is professed by nearly three-quarters of Sudan's citizens. A substantial minority—perhaps as much as 10 percent—continue in traditional, tribal faiths. Growing numbers of these are turning to Christianity.

CHURCH LIFE

Coptic Christians lived in the area as early as the fourth century. Today Sudan is home to several million Christians; it is estimated that they number as much as 20 percent of the population of Sudan. They live mainly in the south (of which

80 percent is estimated to be Christian). Despite enormous persecution, they have been able to carry out significant ministry programs. Crusades have been held in the capital city of Khartoum, and churches have multiplied rapidly in the south. Several foreign agencies, despite the significant danger, provide humanitarian aid, literature, and training.

PERSECUTION

The National Islamic Front's (NIF) forced Islamization campaign, directed primarily against black African Christians and animists in south Sudan, continues as one of the most vicious attacks on the church worldwide. There is ongoing documentation of Christians being sold into slavery to Arab traders from north Sudan, of families being torn apart, of children being forced to embrace Islam, of churches being destroyed, of torture, and even reports of Christians being "crucified" by being tied to crosses and beaten. The NIF regime's use of starvation as a weapon of war in the fifteen-year civil conflict has brought widespread suffering and death. Over the past several years, nine Roman Catholic institutions have been demolished or confiscated. Pastors have been arrested and imprisoned on contrived charges, while Muslim converts to Christianity have been arrested and sentenced to death.

Bishop Henry was consecrated in 1988 as bishop of the Wau diocese in Sudan. He is about sixty years old and married with four children. His first wife was taken and wedded to a Muslim while he was studying in the United Kingdom for a year.

Bishop Henry has been arrested and jailed on false charges not once but twice. Even so, he sees the four-plus years he spent in prison as God's way of making him a blessing to his inmates by sharing his faith, praying, and encouraging the disheartened. Some inmates gave their lives to Christ, including a few Muslims. About one hundred and fifty were baptized by visiting pastors, and not one Christian was hanged during a prison term.

Bishop Henry was first arrested in 1994 after helping to start the relief organization Save Sudanese from Disaster and Care for Children (SSDCC). The trumped-up charges, instigated by former trustees who worked for the government, led to a three-year prison sentence. Four months into the prison term, Bishop Henry and another leader of the organization appealed the decision and were found not guilty. They were released and all charges against them were dropped.

Another bishop, who happened to be a minister in the cabinet of the government of Sudan, dreaded to see them free and used all his power to get Bishop Henry behind bars again. He succeeded, and in 1996 Bishop Henry was arrested on the same charges as before. He appealed again, and the case was finally dropped in early 1999 due to a lack of evidence; however, not before he had spent more than four years in prison.

When Bishop Henry was first imprisoned, he was put in a private, comfortable cell, with flushing toilet, ceiling fan, and a shower. He felt lonely, however, and longed to have fellowship with others, so he asked to be transferred to the main prison. He knew he would have give up all these luxuries, but he persisted.

One day around Easter 1997, while Bishop Henry was sitting in the prison chapel, two Muslim men approached him saying that they had given their lives to Christ. Realizing that they could be informers, he politely asked them to tell him how it happened. Jaali said there were no dreams or anything spectacular— he simply found himself being drawn to Christ and thus gave his life to Him. El Gasim's story, on the other hand, did involve visions. He said that one day while bowing down in prayer, praying the usual five times a day, he saw the sign of the cross. He would change positions but the cross wouldn't go away. This went on for seven days. He had no explanation for it except that Christ was calling him to give his life to Him.

Bishop Henry was very excited upon hearing this and explained to El Gasim that the cross signifies his salvation, and whoever accepts Christ as his Savior will have eternal life, and if he repents, his sins are forgiven. He also explained that living for Christ will not be without suffering. They prayed together. Other Muslim inmates saw them praying together and reported them to the authorities. When summoned to the superintendent's office, they openly declared their faith in Christ and received twenty-five lashes each, administered by a Christian warder. Upon further interrogation, Jaali renounced his Christian faith, saying that he was a Muslim and only interested in knowing what Christianity was all about. El Gasim confessed Christ and said he would face the consequence no matter what. This enraged the authorities. He was beaten, shackled in heavy chains, and put on death row to be hanged.

When Bishop Henry saw El Gasim again, weighed down by the heavy chains on his feet, he heard about all that had happened to him and how he had suffered for his Christian faith. Bishop Henry had great compassion on El Gasim, knowing that if God did not intervene, he was surely staring death in the eye. The bishop encouraged him, citing Paul and Silas' story, reminding him that he wouldn't be the first to be beaten and chained for the sake of Christ. The important thing to remember was that Paul and Silas prayed and praised God, then their chains fell off and the prison doors opened. Bishop Henry confirmed that it could still happen today because the power that worked then—in Acts 16:25–30—was still at work today. They prayed together, earnestly seeking God's will.

Bishop Henry retired to his room and continued praying. In the meantime, El Gasim, who felt encouraged by the bishop's words, took the first step, and, to his surprise, the unexpected happened—the chain broke loose and fell from his leg. Bystanders, whose attention was drawn by the sound of the falling chain, watched in amazement as he took a second step—and the same thing happened. A miracle had occurred right before them. El Gasim went to the warder and told him, "Your chains are in the chapel; go and collect them."

Trembling and confused, the warder informed his superiors of this strange occurrence. An emergency meeting was convened. The incident could not be ignored or excused as nonsense; there were too many witnesses. After careful consideration, they decided it best to let El Gasim go free, because if he stayed he would certainly convert others to Christianity. They realized that it wouldn't help to send him to another prison, because even there they wouldn't be able to stop Christ from doing miracles.

The bishop rejoiced with El Gasim upon his release. While in prison, many inmates, and especially those on death row, called on Bishop Henry for prayer and encouragement. He baptized one man hours before he was to be hanged, reminding him that those who are in Christ Jesus are not under condemnation, even if their bodies are killed. The man's sentence was temporarily revoked.

Bishop Henry felt that while he was in prison things changed for the better. The congregation grew from thirty to one hundred and fifty people. Some Muslims told him that once they were released, they would become Christians, for in prison they were afraid of being mistreated or even killed. Later, his wife told him that she felt his imprisonment was permitted by God not only to be a blessing to his inmates but also for his own safety at the time.

THE FUTURE

Despite the hardship and persecution, the church continues to grow. At the present rate, it will form a major part of the country early this century, reaching well over one-third of the population by 2050. Unfortunately, it is unlikely peace will be had until Christians are the majority, and the greater the number of Christians the more ruthless the government's persecution is likely to be. This persecution will slow growth somewhat.

PRAYERS FOR THE SUFFERING

1. *Christian leaders cannot work due to hunger and disease.* If outside help could be fully restored and aid goods could reach the Sudanese church, their ability to evangelize and make converts would be substantially increased. Pray for increased assistance to the Sudanese church to be made possible.

2. *The church suffers from the military conflict.* There seems to be little the outside world can do to stop the warfare in Sudan, short of direct military intervention. Pray for God to divinely move in Sudan in order to bring about the peace the world cannot achieve.

3. *The church suffers from disagreement over the conduct of the war.* Many Christians are involved in the war for independence against the north. There is considerable disagreement between the factions over military and political matters. Pray for unity in the church itself and for the armies of the south to permit more food aid to the civilians.

4. *The church suffers from a lack of trained leaders*. Due to the rapid expansion of the church and the civil war, the Sudanese church lacks trained leaders and the resources with which to train them. Pray that more training can be provided in order to provide for future growth.

5. *The church suffers from a global lack of interest*. Very few Christians in the world are interested in the church in Sudan; those that might be are often frightened away by the danger of war. Pray that more Christians will move with courage to minister on behalf of their Sudanese brothers and sisters.

6. *Many suffer from enslavement and forced conversion to Islam*. Perhaps one of the greatest atrocities is the continued enslavement of Sudanese Christians. Many Christian leaders around the world differ on their response to this problem. In the past, some have attempted to redeem slaves, but this has been stopped since it was only encouraging many slave traders to continue the practice. Pray that Christians will develop an appropriate and workable response to the slave trade.

7. *The leaders of Sudan suffer from the spiritual blindness covering the land*. The leaders of Sudan are intent upon the total Islamization of the country. Other leaders in our world's history have likewise been determined to proclaim a false god. Pray that God will divinely move to change the hearts of Sudan's leaders, even as He has changed the hearts of past kings.

Please Pray for the Persecuted Church in:

SYRIA

POPULATION 17 million (53% urban)	**CHRISTIANS** 1.2 million, share declining
LAND Southwestern Asia; 71,498 sq. miles (185,180 sq. km)	**PERSECUTION** Isolated, static
LANGUAGES Arabic, Kurdish, Armenian, Aramaic, Circassian	**RESTRICTIONS & FREEDOMS** Freedom of religion
RELIGION 89% Muslim, 7% Christian, 2% nonreligious	**IN THE 21ST CENTURY…** Continued freedom to evangelize will be offset by monitoring and political tension.

Situated in the Middle East between Europe and Israel, Syria consists of a coastal zone divided by a narrow double mountain range from a large eastern region that includes mountains, large desert regions, and the Euphrates River basin. In the southwest corner, these mountains descend into the Golan Heights, an area disputed with Israel.

Syria's seventeen million people for the most part make their home on the coastal plains. They are divided nearly in half between those who live in urban areas and those in rural settlements. About 40 percent are under the age of fifteen. The population includes tens of thousands of Palestinian refugees.

Muslims conquered the area in A.D. 636, and between 660 and 750 the city of Damascus was the center of the important Umayyad Empire. Syria has been ruled by Egyptians, Mongols, and Ottoman Turks.

Most Syrians are farmers. The economy gives Syrians a lower middle income, though growth has been slowed by the worldwide decline in oil prices. The average worker earns a little more than U.S.$500 per year. Although most of the men are literate, only about half of the women are.

The current government is based on a parliamentary constitution enacted in 1973. The president holds much of the power, though the government is theoretically divided between legislative, executive, and judicial spheres. The Alawite minority is the most powerful bloc, even though it forms only a small percentage of the nation's population. The Arab-Israeli conflict has been the primary foreign policy concern of the government.

Nearly 90 percent of Syrians are Muslims, most of whom belong to the Sunni branch. About 13 percent are Alawites. Some 2 percent of the population professes to be nonreligious, while the remainder is generally associated with Christianity.

CHURCH LIFE

There were apparently Christians in Syria before the conversion of the apostle Paul, who was on his way to Damascus when he was converted. After the fall of Jerusalem, Antioch became the center of eastern Christianity. Antioch's theologians played an important role in the controversies of the early church. The Greek Orthodox Church claims history back to these ancient times, but

Catholics and Protestants have been in Syria only since the 1700s. The influence of Western Christianity has been strong, particularly since 1890, in large part due to the influence of Christian schools on the ruling leaders.

PERSECUTION

The regime of Syrian General and President Hafiz Al-Assad sought to divorce the state from any religious commitment at all. This trend toward secularization has resulted in religious riots instigated by conservatives. Although Christian churches are legally recognized, and Islam is not the religion of the state, Islam is given a position of importance. Freedom of religion exists to some degree, solemn processions are authorized, and new religious buildings can be constructed. Syrian law even permits children to change their religion upon coming of age (usually not the case under Islamic law). Christians are permitted to witness so long as they do not disrupt government or community harmony; they are often watched, and even though they have freedom many find it difficult to evangelize under the circumstances.

THE FUTURE

By the middle of the next century the church in Syria could more than double in size, perhaps even reaching four million in number. However, the growth of the church is still not keeping up with the overall population, so the church's share in Syria is actually slowly declining (due in part to emigration).

PRAYERS FOR THE SUFFERING

1. *The church enjoys enormous freedom.* Unfortunately, many have found it difficult to capitalize on the opportunity. Converts from Islam have been few and far between. Pray that the church will be bold in its witness.

2. *The church enjoys the respect of Syria.* Believers are an influential minority in most of the cities, industries, professions, and military. This respect has given them an opportunity to reach out; pray that they will utilize this time to share the gospel.

3. *The church suffers from false perceptions among Muslims.* Many Muslims have wrong ideas about Christianity. Pray that new contacts between Christians and Muslims will help to correct misunderstandings and false perceptions.

4. *The church enjoys freedom to distribute and sell evangelistic literature.* The *Jesus* film is widely available, and bookstores are operated. Pray that these stores will be frequented by Muslims and that the current brisk sales and distribution will continue.

Please Pray for the Persecuted Church in:

TAJIKISTAN

POPULATION	**PERSECUTION**
6.1 million (32% urban)	Isolated, growing
LAND	**RESTRICTIONS & FREEDOMS**
Central Asia, landlocked; 55,251 sq. miles (143,100 sq. km)	Freedom of religion
LANGUAGES	**IN THE 21ST CENTURY...** The church must work quickly to increase its growth rate in order to prevent the further erosion of its position.
Tajik, Russian	
RELIGION	
90% Muslim	
CHRISTIANS	
130,000, share rapidly declining	

The nation of Tajikistan, located in Central Asia, is dominated by the Pamir and Alay mountain chains. A dense network of rivers cuts valleys through the mountain chains, where pastureland can be found. Some of the mountains are high enough to have year-round snows and glaciers.

Some six million people are estimated to reside in Tajikistan, of which 41 percent are under the age of fifteen. There are many different ethnic groups including Iranians, Russians, Ukrainians, Germans, and Armenians. The official state language is Tajik, but Russian is widely used in government and business.

Tajikistan has been occupied for much of its past, from the twelfth century under the Persians to the nineteenth century under the Russians. When the Soviet Empire collapsed, civil war broke out, which was finally resolved in 1993.

Today, Tajikistan is a republic. Its national government has centered nearly all administrative powers in the executive branch. The head of the government is the prime minister, and the system continues to be dominated by the Communist Party.

Tajikistan is a poor nation, with a gross national product of U.S.$470 per capita. The economy is evenly split between agriculture, industry, and services. Although unemployment is low, the economy has continued to decline; the principal crop is cotton, which has suffered from a worldwide fall in prices. Virtually all of the adults are literate, and schooling is compulsory. Health care has declined in quality since independence, and increasing pollution has led to increasing disease.

The large majority of Tajiks are Muslims. A very small minority of people adhere to Christianity or other traditional religions.

CHURCH LIFE

Christianity came to Tajikistan during the early centuries, brought by workers with the Apostolic Church of the East. Tamerlane's armies decimated it, and Islam came to fill the spiritual vacuum that followed. Today, 4 percent of the population in Tajikistan is Christian. Churches are being built and evangelism is seeing response, but much remains to be done. The largest bloc of Christians are the Russian Orthodox.

PERSECUTION

Although there is freedom of religion in Tajikistan, there is opposition from local Muslims. The spread of Islam is supported by Iranian propaganda and, on occasion, by Afghani soldiers. And, in many cases, Tajiks who embrace Christianity experience the fiercest opposition from their own families.

That's what nineteen-year-old Zarina experienced when she accepted Jesus Christ as her Savior. At first she felt an overwhelming peace and an immediate release from the bondage she had known trying to follow the rules and duties of growing up in a strict Muslim family. But then the gravity of her decision hit her. She knew her family would not understand why she had turned from Islam.

Zarina kept her new faith private for six months, reading her Bible in secret and slipping away on Sundays in order to attend underground church services. Finally, when her family announced she was to be married in an arranged wedding, she proclaimed her faith in Christ. Her grandfather immediately started to beat her, only stopping fifteen minutes later due to an asthma attack. The beatings continued the next day, this time from Zarina's father, a former soldier in Afghanistan who had been out of town. He locked Zarina in her room, saying, "You will never leave until you repent."

Over the next six months, mullahs from the mosque visited Zarina, praying for her and pressuring her to return to Islam, but she resisted. Her father reached the breaking point. "Zarina, you have five minutes before I kill you. Who do you choose? Your family or Jesus?"

Zarina recalls, "I was so tired and so broken. I was down to my last ounce of faith." Still, she found the resolve to say, "Jesus is my Savior."

For the next two hours Zarina was beaten by the father she loved. All she could do was to sob and endure the strikes, all the time wondering how her family could suddenly hate her so much. Her father then pushed her outside and into the car. He threw a shovel into the backseat and announced that he was going to bury her alive. The only thing that stopped him was realizing that there were still two days left of Ramadan, the Islamic holy month in which Muslims are not to sin. Zarina was brought inside the house. She remembers silently praying, "Jesus, I will be with you soon."

The next day Zarina happened to be near a phone when it rang. The caller, a Christian friend, whispered, "Zarina, I will be waiting at the bus stop tomorrow. Meet me there." Before she could respond, the friend hung up. Despite the terrible beatings, Zarina didn't want to leave. She loved her family and wanted them to accept her and, eventually, accept Christ.

The next day Zarina found herself uncharacteristically alone in the house. She wandered around praying until she finally decided to meet the friend. She walked slowly away from her house, almost hoping someone would stop her. No one did. After meeting the friend and hiding in a nearby village for three months, Jesus revealed to her much about His faithfulness and love. After much prayer, she decided that she needed to reconcile with her family.

When Zarina returned home, everyone rejoiced—everyone, that is, except her father who was away on business. Her mother told Zarina that he had suffered the most, ashamed of what he had done to his own daughter. Even so, when he arrived the next day, his first words to Zarina were, "I hate you. My daughter died three months ago."

Zarina fell at his feet, crying as she hugged his legs. "My God told me to come back," she said. "I will never leave you. You can beat me. You can kill me, but I will never leave." With those words, her father broke down and hugged Zarina.

For the next nine months, an uneasy truce existed. Zarina's family accepted her Christianity as long as she kept it private. She began working for a Christian organization whose leaders encouraged her to go to Bible college in the United States. Zarina was excited for the opportunity but desired her father's blessing, so important in the Tajik culture. When she asked him, she covered her eyes, not wanting to see his reaction. Surprisingly, he calmly asked, "Are you sure you want to study this Jesus?" When she said yes, he responded, "You do what you think is right."

And now, after devoting herself to Bible classes and learning more about Christ, Zarina is hoping to return soon to Central Asia, this time to war-torn Afghanistan, to minister to her Muslim sisters and share Christ's love with them.

THE FUTURE

The church is presently declining slowly; set in the context of rapid population growth, its part in the country as a whole is facing rapid erosion. It could very well number less than 100,000 members by 2050. The decline is caused in large part by the emigration of Russian Orthodox.

PRAYERS FOR THE SUFFERING

1. *The church is enjoying a limited window of freedom.* Pray that this window may be used to the maximum effect.

2. *The church must acquire a Tajik face.* Christianity has been dominated for years by the culture of Russian and Ukrainian Orthodox. Now it must become integrated into the Tajik society. Pray that this is accomplished with wisdom.

3. *Large numbers of Tajiks have turned to Christianity in Afghanistan.* Pray that some of these will be able to help plant the church in Tajikistan and that a move toward Christ would occur in this nation.

Please Pray for the Persecuted Church in:

TUNISIA

POPULATION
9.5 million (63% urban)

LAND
Northern Africa; 63,170 sq. miles (163,610 sq. km)

LANGUAGES
Arabic, French

RELIGION
99% Muslim

CHRISTIANS
50,000, growing

PERSECUTION
Harassment, growing

RESTRICTIONS & FREEDOMS
Freedom to worship
Evangelism possible but limited
Islamic fundamentalism a growing force

IN THE 21ST CENTURY...
Although the number of Tunisian believers initially will be small, it has the potential to begin growing exponentially in later decades.

Tunisia is a small country situated between Libya and Algeria. Its northern mountains (some of which are nearly a mile high) are dotted with fertile valleys and plains. The hills give way to a plateau in the south that descends gradually into a chain of salt lakes. The southern half joins the Sahara Desert. Tunisia has a Mediterranean climate in the north, but it gradually gets hotter and drier further south.

Nine and a half million people live in Tunisia, two-thirds in the cities. Tunis, the capital, is also the largest city with nearly 700,000 residents. Moreover, three-quarters of the population live in the coastal areas; although the southern deserts comprise 70 percent of the land area, they account for only 30 percent of its population. The people are mostly Arabs with some Berber and European minorities. One-third are under the age of fifteen. Education is free, and the University of Tunis has more than 110,000 students; despite this, more than half of all adults have no formal schooling and only two-thirds are literate.

As with most of the countries in North Africa, the economy of Tunisia is dominated by oil. Unemployment and underemployment are both significant problems, unemployment being estimated at more than 13 percent. The average worker earns about U.S.$2,000 per year.

In the earliest part of its history, 800 years before Christ, Tunisia was founded as part of the Carthaginian juggernaut by Phoenician traders. By 200 B.C. the

Romans conquered and made Tunisia part of the empire, and Christianity came to the area shortly after the time of Christ. In the seventh century, Muslim armies took Tunisia, along with most of North Africa. The Muslims eradicated most of Christianity, and had several hundred years of rule before clashes began with Europe. Pirates based in Tunisia harried European traffic for years, but they were sharply curtailed by the United States Navy in the 1800s. With the loss of the pirate trade came a steep financial downturn that sparked general unrest; French military troops entered Tunisia in 1880 and made the country a protectorate in 1883. French influence permeated the nation and left a strong mark, but nationalism eventually led to Tunisia's independence in 1956. In the first years of its new government it declared itself a republic and clashed violently with France several times, but eventually stability was reached and Tunisia continued to tighten its ties with the Arab world. Today, Tunisia is a republic with a president, prime minister, and a national assembly.

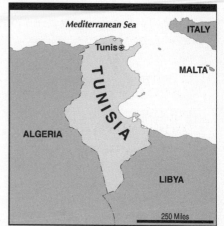

Virtually all Tunisians are Muslims, most of the Sunni tradition. There are minorities of Jews and Christians. Kairouan, a holy city and a place of pilgrimage, is famous as an Islamic center.

CHURCH LIFE

Christianity was first brought to Tunisia around the end of the first century and was deeply hurt by the Donatist schism. Although Islam swept the area in the seventh century, Christianity survived for another 300 years. A new church was planted by the Franciscans and the Dominicans in the thirteenth century. Today there are more than 50,000 Christians in Tunisia, the large majority of whom are expatriate French Catholics and Lebanese refugees. There are only a few thousand Tunisian Christians, and they are often isolated, fearful, untrained in their faith, and prone to backslide.

PERSECUTION

The constitution proclaims Islam to be the state religion and stipulates that the chief of state must be a Muslim. It guarantees freedom of conscience and protects the free exercise of worship. These stances have been tempered in the face of increasing Islamic fundamentalism, and though the government tolerates Christian worship, it is not favorable toward evangelism. Although there is little overt, harsh persecution, Islam has permeated the society and erected significant cultural barriers to conversion.

A believer writes: "The year 1997 was a bad one for our church. The government started a large-scale investigation into converts with many arrests and interrogations. The church has not truly recovered from this. We are full of fear. Unless we overcome this, we cannot expect growth. We need to be bold. We have only a few house churches and there is very little trust amongst the Christians."

THE FUTURE

The church has a certain amount of freedom and, where this is true, it is able to experience some growth. Current trends suggest the church could more than double in size by 2050 and that it will increase its share of the overall population (its growth rate is outstripping that of the country as a whole). It is likely that as it grows it will incur additional restrictions from the vocal Muslim majority. Perhaps the most significant challenge of the future is the need to train leaders to support this coming growth.

PRAYERS FOR THE SUFFERING

1. *The church enjoys limited freedom.* Pray that Tunisian believers will use this window of opportunity to broadly evangelize the land.

2. *Observers worry about rising Islamic fundamentalism.* Pray that this tide will be reduced and that there will be continuing good relations between Christian and Muslim leaders, in order to keep persecution in check.

Please Pray for the Persecuted Church in:

TURKEY

POPULATION 66.5 million (71% urban)	**PERSECUTION** Sporadic, growing
LAND Southeastern Europe and Southwestern Asia; 300,948 sq. miles (779,452 sq. km)	**RESTRICTIONS & FREEDOMS** Freedom to worship Discreet evangelism possible
LANGUAGES Turkish, Kurdish, Arabic	**IN THE 21ST CENTURY...** The church will continue to have difficulties challenging the strong grip of Islam,
RELIGION 97% Muslim	but this effort will have strategic importance for
CHRISTIANS 373,000, declining	much of the Middle East.

Placed in a strategic location between Europe and the Middle East, Turkey has been a crossroads for many ancient peoples. At one time, these famous routes featured constant caravans carrying silk and spices from China.

The population has reached sixty-six million people, with almost 40 percent under the age of fifteen.

During the Middle Ages (A.D. 500–1500), Turkish nomads roamed Central Asia and Mongolia, living in tents and worshiping nature. In the sixth century they overran Mongolia. Their character changed as they came into contact with Arab Muslims; they began to assimilate Islam into their own religion. As the Arabs declined in power, a strong Turkish clan called the Seljuks conquered Persia, creating a new empire and eventually dominating the whole of the Middle East. As they did, the Roman Catholic Church launched military attacks against them. These "Crusades" left a trail of death, destruction, and abandoned fortresses, and impressed upon the Turkish people a terribly distorted image of the church.

Finally the Mongols swept through the area and toppled the Seljuks from power. Modern-day Turkey, then called Anatolia, became home to many returning Turks and was eventually divided into ten states. Out of these rose the Ottoman Empire, which flourished throughout the region. After more than three centuries of power and influence, the empire grew stagnant; civil unrest led to the formation of underground resistance groups to reform Turkey's structure. During World War I, the empire sided with Germany. Afterward, Turkish nationalists drove back a Greek invasion and forced the Allies to establish the modern Republic of Turkey. The new country reformed the laws, alphabet, and governing system, to be in line with European norms.

Turkey is agriculturally self-sufficient; tourism and industry are both critical parts of its economy. Its growing ties with the nations of Central Asia are an important part of its long-term strategy for regional influence and economic stability. Turkey is one of the poorest nations in Europe; workers have an average income of U.S.$1,400 per year.

Although Turkey is a secular state, Muslims continue to dominate its culture. Most are Sunnis, although there are a minority of Shia's.

CHURCH LIFE

From a substantial Christian base, Turkey has all but eliminated its Christian population. Turks have long-standing bitter memories, slanted perceptions, and wrong ideas about the church. Yet, against these substantial barriers, an indigenous Turkish church has been planted.

PERSECUTION

Some Christians have been arrested but all have been released. Believers face more persecution from societal pressure. Legal recognition is not impossible but is very slow. Some expatriates have been expelled from the country, but if done discreetly, evangelism is possible.

A recent wave of harassment hit the church on September 12, 1999, as Turkish police barged into Izmir Fellowship of Jesus Christ in the middle of their Sunday morning service. Not only did the Christians have to deal with the police invasion, they were also subjected to a TV camera crew filming their ordeal as the officers proceeded to arrest forty members of the fellowship. Those who were arrested (including five foreigners), were then carted off to the police station. They were held overnight and were subjected to interrogation by the Terrorism Bureau. In spite of this, the believers showed great spirit. Just like Paul and Silas, they sang together—praising God from the confines of their cells. The singing, however, did not go down well with the guards, who yelled at them to shut up.

"We were treated as criminal suspects," one of the Christians said, "but I refused to state my crime. I had not committed any crime."

The pastor of the church believed the arrests were part of a news-making exercise by the tabloid media. "Unfortunately, certain media groups, in an effort to create sensational news, have opposed our beliefs in an aggressive and disrespectful manner." The Christians' ordeal was featured as an "exclusive" item on Turkish news that very evening.

The Izimir Christians are now forbidden to worship in their building. Instead, they are caught up in a court case that could involve them in tedious legal wrangling for many months to come.

Other Christians—this time in Istanbul—have been through an ordeal similar to that of their brothers and sisters in Izmir. On October 3, 1999, police raided a service at the Zeytinburnu Fellowship of Jesus Christ. The police rounded up all but a handful of the believers. Those who remained—the young mothers with their children and a few elderly people—watched, powerless, as their family and friends were taken away.

Elders of the fellowship were dismayed when the security police accused them of meeting without proper authorization. They, too, had done all they could to inform the appropriate officials about their meetings when they purchased their church building six years ago. One of the leaders said, "Our city authorities have even recognized our legal right to exemption from utility charges, just like other churches and all mosques in the country. So why are they now deciding we are illegal?"

THE FUTURE

The church is in decline largely due to the emigration of Armenians, Greeks, and Assyrians. The indigenous Turkish church is growing but numbers less than 1,000. By 2050 Turkish believers could number in the tens of thousands, but the total number of Christians in Turkey will likely stand at only a hundred thousand.

PRAYERS FOR THE SUFFERING

1. *The church needs courage to stand.* Persecution has been sporadic, and at this time there seems to be little severe danger despite reports of harassment.

2. *The church has an image problem.* Long-standing memories need to be met with new ministries of healing and reconciliation. Some of these have already begun; pray for their ongoing success.

3. *The church is enjoying growth in some areas, but enduring decline over-all.* The Turkish church must move into prominence and be supported with training and discipleship programs. Pray for unity among Turkish leaders.

4. *Missionaries are generally not permitted in Turkey.* However, expatriates can make a significant impact through correspondence, short-term trips, and other avenues. Pray that more Christians will take an interest in this nation.

Please Pray for the Persecuted Church in:

TURKMENISTAN

POPULATION	**PERSECUTION**
4.4 million (45% urban)	Harassment, static
LAND	**RESTRICTIONS & FREEDOMS**
Central Asia, 188,456 sq. miles (488,100 sq. km)	Limited freedom to evangelize
LANGUAGES	**IN THE 21ST CENTURY...**
Turkmen, Russian, Uzbek	The number of Turkmen believers will probably con-
RELIGION	tinue to be very small, and the size of the church will
75% Muslim	flux with the size of the
CHRISTIANS	expatriate community.
98,000, declining rapidly	

Turkmenistan is located in Central Asia, bordering the Caspian Sea, between Iran and Kazakhstan. It is made up of flat, rolling deserts with dunes rising to mountains in the south.

There are over four million people living in Turkmenistan. A third of the population is under the age of fifteen; nearly half live in cities. Three-quarters are Turkmen, but there are significant minorities of Russians and Uzbeks, as well as other ethnic groups. The largest city and capital is Ashkhabad, home to about 400,000.

The government is a republic but is not yet completely stable, and political freedom is not universal. Turkmenistan won its independence on October 27, 1991, and adopted a constitution on May 18, 1992.

Turkmenistan is primarily made up of desert country with nomadic cattle raising, intensive agriculture in irrigated oases, and huge gas and oil resources. It is the world's tenth largest producer of cotton and possesses the fifth largest reserves of natural gas, as well as substantial oil resources. Thus, most people work either in agriculture or petroleum; unemployment is very low and the economy has been growing each year. Nearly everyone is literate and educated. Although access to advanced technology is minimal, basic services (such as health and shelter) are well taken care of.

Three-quarters of the population are Muslim; the remaining 25 percent hold to ancient superstitions or have declared themselves nonreligious.

CHURCH LIFE

Like most of Asia, Christianity spread in Turkmenistan through the Apostolic Church of the East but was largely wiped out by the armies of Timur (Tamerlane). Islam swept through the area and came to dominate it. Today only 2 percent of the population is Christian. Although gains are being made by Catholics, Protestants, and independent churches, significant losses are being felt by the Orthodox churches as many of their members emigrate back to Russia. A large majority of Turkmenistan's Christians remain secret believers.

PERSECUTION

There have been martyrs in Turkmenistan in the past; however, there is some freedom to evangelize. At the same time, Christians have been harassed by Muslims and face some restrictions by the government. Rahim Tashov, for example, pastors a Baptist church in Turkmenabad. He has been trying to register his church for many months but has been told verbally that the authorities would never allow a Protestant church to be registered in Turkmenistan. The pressure has been constant. Rahim's church was raided not long ago, and he was detained overnight. Three months later, two female teachers from his church were fired from their jobs, and one of them was banned from visiting Rahim's home. Over the last months, children attending the church's Sunday school have been singled out for disgrace in their schools and banned from visiting Christians.

In the latest move, Turkmen authorities once again arrested Rahim and interrogated him. He was given a "final warning" not to gather people in any place for Christian activities or they would be put in prison.

Shagildy Atakov has also suffered for his faith. On March 19, 1999, he was sentenced to two years in a labor camp for alleged swindling in his car-trading business. But Shagildy was innocent. A Russian human rights activist explained, "This is a common practice of the Turkmen authorities. They try not to use political charges against prisoners of conscience, but they send them to prison for ordinary criminal offenses."

The *real* truth is, Shagildy, a Turkmen convert to Christianity, was a very active preacher in his church. Before his arrest, he had been visited and threatened several times by various state officials including a secret police officer, a religious affairs committee representative, and the local senior imam (Muslim prayer leader).

On August 3, Shagildy was retried—after the authorities decided his initial two-year sentence was too lenient. He was sentenced to four years in a labor camp. His family has also said he has been singled out for harsh punishment in the prison. When they visited him, Shagildy could not let them embrace him because his body hurt too much.

In the latest twist to the tale, Shagildy's wife and five children were forcibly removed from their home on February 3, 2000, and transported to his parents' house, 120 miles away.

Further victims include Shagildy's brother, Chariyar, and Baptist church leader Anatoly Belayev. On April 17, 1999, they were stopped at a police checkpoint and a cargo of Turkmen Bibles was discovered in their car. The two men were interrogated—Chariyar was severely beaten—and locked in a cold cell for the night. The next day they were dumped outside the city.

Just before dawn on December 17, 1999, the police came for Anatoly again. He was released after six hours in detention but rearrested in early February. At the time of this writing, he remains in detention.

THE FUTURE

The church's share of the population is declining very rapidly. By 2050 it will have probably fallen to less than 80,000 members, numbering less than 1 percent of the populace, and will continue to be marginalized in the society.

PRAYERS FOR THE SUFFERING

1. *The church suffers from a lack of broad foundations.* Pray for the firm establishment of the Turkmen church, capable of spreading the gospel throughout Turkmenistan and of attracting large numbers of Turkmen believers.

2. *The church enjoys limited freedom.* Pray that this window of opportunity will be used and that it will continue to increase.

3. *The church needs to continually work to enhance its image and gain the respect of the populace.* Pray for new opportunities for Christians to improve

good relations between the church and the government, perhaps through compassionate relief and community development.

4. *The church enjoys substantial global interest.* Praise God for the large partnership devoted to the evangelization of the Turkmen peoples. Pray that foreign missionaries will find significant opportunities to partner with Turkmen believers to see the gospel preached. Pray that the global body of Christ will take advantage of the current window of opportunity to provide the Turkmen church with significant resources for evangelism and to support them with additional evangelistic programs (including shortwave radio and TV broadcasts).

Please Pray for the Persecuted Church in:

UZBEKISTAN

POPULATION 24.3 million (41% urban)	**PERSECUTION** Harassment, growing
LAND Central Asia, 172,742 sq. miles (447,400 sq. km)	**RESTRICTIONS & FREEDOMS** Muslims may not convert Christians have different identity cards
LANGUAGES Uzbek, Russian	Converts may be arrested, imprisoned, ostracized
RELIGION 95% Muslim	**IN THE 21ST CENTURY...** The Christian community,
CHRISTIANS 400,000, share declining very rapidly	largely expatriate, will con- tinue in a state of significant flux.

U zbekistan is located in Central Asia. Its land is mostly sandy desert dotted with dunes surrounding flat, intensely irrigated river valleys along the courses of the Amu Darya, the Sirdaryo, and the Zarashon. More than half of the land is used for agriculture, most for raising cattle.

About twenty-four million people live in Uzbekistan, one-third of whom are under the age of fifteen. Major cities include Tashkent, Samarkand, and Bukhara, all of which have centuries of history.

Uzbekistan was part of the Soviet Union until its collapse in the 1990s. They gained their independence on August 31, 1991. Their new constitution was adopted December 8, 1992, but is still undergoing much change. The current government is an evolution of Soviet civil law and still lacks an independent judicial system.

Uzbekistan is a dry, landlocked country. It was one of the poorest areas of the Soviet Union with more than 60 percent of its population living in densely populated rural communities. Uzbekistan is now the third largest cotton exporter, a major producer of gold and natural gas, and a regionally significant producer of chemicals and machinery.

The society of Uzbekistan resembles the West in many ways—the dating process is similar and marriages are not arranged. The average family has five members. Nearly all Uzbeks can read and write. Telephones, televisions, and other media are widely available.

More than two-thirds of the population are Muslims. Many practice superstitious beliefs with a thin veneer of Islam on top, often wearing charms and holding to animistic faiths.

CHURCH LIFE

Christianity first spread into Central Asia with the Apostolic Church of the East, but was largely wiped out through the military campaigns of Tamerlane. In the centuries afterward, Islam moved into the wasteland; today Christianity claims about 2 percent of the population. About half of these are secret believers, and most of the remainder are Russian Orthodox who moved into the area during the period of the Soviet Union. Many of the latter are leaving the country rapidly as Russians return home. This wave of emigration has led to the rapid decline of the church in Uzbekistan.

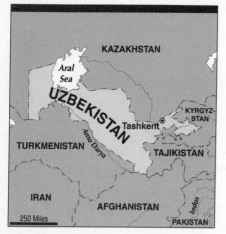

PERSECUTION

There is no evidence of any formally state-sponsored persecution of Christians. However, a special commission organized by the government has found grave violations of human rights by individual Uzbek security agents who have, in recent years, resorted to planting drugs on fundamentalist Muslims, political activists, and evangelical Christians, as a pretext to arrest and convict them on false charges. Only registered churches are permitted to function; the government does not permit any independent forms of religion. All forms of outreach are generally forbidden, and Christian leaders are often under surveillance and harassed.

In 1999, Christians from an ethnic Muslim background were jailed in Nukus, and a pastor was arrested, tortured, and sentenced to two years of labor for holding "unsanctioned" church meetings. Four Christian pastors were also arrested on falsified drug charges and received stiff jail terms of five to fifteen years. In the wake of widespread international protests, President Islam Karimov ordered the four released, along with another Uzbek pastor jailed on a one-year sentence for Christian evangelism activities.

Another Christian Uzbek pastor was recently jailed on contrived fraud charges. Pastor Kim Stanislav of the Chilchik Christian Church did not receive a formal trial and his lawyer was not allowed to be present at the court proceedings.

An Uzbek citizen of Korean descent, Stanislav was directing a local construction company when he embraced Christianity in the early 1990s, church sources said. Stanislav received a three-and-a-half-year prison sentence for what his congregation says are falsified charges of tax fraud by the construction company he directed before he resigned to become a full-time pastor.

"This brother had a strong witness through his vocation," a personal acquaintance said, "and he led many to Christ." But local municipal authorities, including the mayor of Chilchik, forced the businessman's resignation as director of the Chilchik Construction Company after he started pastoring the Chilchik Christian Church, an independent congregation meeting in house church fellowships. At least one-quarter of the 200-member congregation are ethnic Uzbeks.

When Stanislav refused to renounce his Christian activities, he was reportedly threatened that unless he paid a massive $5,000 bribe, he would be arrested and thrown in jail. "He was too honest," one source commented. "And until now he has refused to allow any publicity about his jailing because he personally wanted to stay and minister inside the prison." Stanislav reportedly led twenty-five of his cellmates to Christ during his first month of imprisonment. When he was offered the comfort of a private cell after being sentenced, he declined so that he could continue sharing his faith and discipling other prisoners.

THE FUTURE

The present decline of the church will possibly stabilize around 2025 with about 1 percent of the nation, and then begin to increase in number. By 2050 it is probable that Christians in the land will number between 300,000 and 400,000, many of whom will be secret believers.

PRAYERS FOR THE SUFFERING

1. *The Uzbek church does not yet have an indigenous identity of its own.* Pray for the Uzbek church to be able to develop its own character and to use evangelism and new converts to reverse the decline caused by emigration.

2. *The church endures only moderate restrictions.* Praise God for the limited freedoms afforded the church by the government. Pray that the security forces will cease their harassment of the church.

3. *Pastors are sporadically targeted for harassment.* Praise God for the boldness of Uzbek pastors, and pray for their protection from persecution.

4. *The church enjoys a substantial amount of interest from foreign missions.* Praise God for the large partnership devoted to ministry in Central Asia. Pray that they will continue to find new ways to support the church in Uzbekistan with evangelistic and discipleship resources.

Please Pray for the Persecuted Church in:

VIETNAM

POPULATION 79.8 million (19% urban)	**PERSECUTION** Sharp, but sporadic improvement
LAND Southeastern Asia; 127,428 sq. miles (330,036 sq. km)	**RESTRICTIONS & FREEDOMS** Limited evangelism
LANGUAGES Vietnamese, French, Chinese, English, Khmer, indigenous	**IN THE 21ST CENTURY...** Religious freedom and opportunities will grow slowly, accompanied by isolated but regular and highly visible bouts of sharp persecution.
RELIGION 50% Buddhist	
CHRISTIANS 6.5 million, share growing rapidly	

Vietnam is located in Southeast Asia: a low, flat delta in the south and north, with hills in the center and mountains in the far north and northwest.

There are nearly eighty million people living in Vietnam. A third of them are under the age of fifteen. About 20 percent live in cities, while the remainder live in smaller rural villages. Nearly all are Vietnamese; there are small minority ethnic groups, including Chinese.

The nation has been torn and wounded, with many scars from many different sources. Vietnam has known little but warfare and hardship since 1941, partly caused by the creation of a Communist state in 1945. After some three decades North Vietnam conquered the South in 1975 and battled Cambodia from 1978 to 1985.

A Communist government controls Vietnam. The legal system is based on a mix of Communist theory and French civil law. Although liberties are still restricted, the nation is slowly opening up to the rest of the world.

The country is economically poor due to the ravages of conflict and the loss of financial support from the Soviet bloc, and there are many opportunities for ministries devoted to community development and relief. Diseases such as cholera are prevalent.

About half the people practice Buddhism. A small minority follows new Asian religions or old animistic beliefs.

CHURCH LIFE

Vietnam's church is in a minority position, making up about 8 percent of the population. About six million are Catholics. The majority of Protestants are now from the tribal minorities, more than half of which have been reached with the gospel. The government has permitted Christian ministries to work in the country, especially in the area of community development and compassionate relief programs.

PERSECUTION

In principle, there is religious freedom in Vietnam. In practice, religious life at the congregational level is generally normal, but at district and national levels, the church is faced with restrictions and difficulties. A 1999 religion decree enshrined religious rights and allowed people to choose to follow, not follow, or change their religion, but warned of punishments for those who used religion to harm the state. Tribal Christians have faced the severest persecution in Vietnam. Said one worker, "The local Party boss has total power over whether a church is burned or stands, and can arbitrarily sentence pastors to short terms of hard labor in the fields." Pastors have been detained under house arrest, and their equipment has been confiscated.

Hmong and the Hre tribal believers have been witnesses (if not the very victims) of countless suffering and persecution. A tribal village in Lam Dong province is home to nearly five hundred people who have become Christians, a church source reports. Their activities are not unknown to the local police. Because of this, Christians in the area have suffered hardship at the hands of the authorities. Quite a number of church leaders and believers have been arrested and many have been fined.

"Four policemen came to the village with a picture of Ho Chi Minh," the source said. "Then they gathered all the known believers in the open field and preached about all the good things that Uncle Ho had done for them and about all the evils of Christianity. They urged all to forsake Christianity and to embrace the teachings of Uncle Ho. Subsequently, they raised a photograph of Ho Chi Minh and ordered all the Christians to bow down in adoration and to show their allegiance to the great leader."

Of the 480 believers gathered, only ten bowed down. These ten later acknowledged what they had done and repented of their sin. Before the police left, they gave a final warning to the group never to worship God or to meet for worship again or they would suffer worse. Then they began to beat those who were standing. There were about twenty men who were beaten, and some were badly hurt. After three days, the believers were surprised to see the head of the local police station apologizing for what his men had done. Sadly, though, he told others a different story. He explained that the people who were beaten were those who refused to pay taxes.

The church source said that when asked how such experiences of persecution affected their Christian lives, these believers responded in simple humility, but in greater faith, that it is not toward men, or any authority, that they should swear allegiance but to the one great and true God, none other than Jesus.

THE FUTURE

The current trend appears to be one of a gradual improvement in relations between the church and the state, coupled with continued attempts at state control. Despite restrictions, the church is presently growing at a faster rate than the population and will likely triple its current size by 2050. By the middle of this century, the church may enjoy even more substantial freedoms than they presently have, particularly if Christians are successful in cultivating a servant relationship with the government of Vietnam.

PRAYERS FOR THE SUFFERING

1. *Believers have suffered in the past from intense persecution.* Thank God for the increasing openness. Pray that the government will expand its policy of permitting Christian ministries to provide compassionate relief, education, and support for orphanages.

2. *The church has suffered from laws restricting their activities.* Praise God for the recent decree allowing greater religious freedom. Pray for the con-

tinued softening of restrictions. Pray especially for the harassment of tribal Christians to be eased.

3. *The nation has suffered from years of war.* Pray for Christian ministries to successfully develop reconciliation and economic development ministries for the people of Vietnam, in order to heal the many scars brought by conflict.

4. *The church is enduring growing pains.* Praise God for the enormous growth of the church. Pray for God to move among Christians, to help provide supportive resources and training for Vietnamese church leaders.

Please Pray for the Persecuted Church in:

YEMEN

Yemen has been described as a land in the twelfth century, racing toward the fifteenth. It is located on the southeastern border of Saudi Arabia, forming a portion of the Arabian Peninsula. It sits on the major mountain range of the southern Arabian Peninsula; the heights separate a small strip of coastal land from the northern deserts. The peaks also form numerous valleys where a wide variety of crops can be grown. Its border with Saudi Arabia remains disputed.

POPULATION
18.1 million (34% urban)

LAND
Southwestern Asia; 203,850 sq. miles (527,968 sq. km)

LANGUAGE
Arabic

RELIGION
99% Muslim

CHRISTIANS
0.5%; share growing

PERSECUTION
Harsh, growing

RESTRICTIONS & FREEDOMS
Conversion can be punished by arrest, imprisonment
No open evangelism permitted
Christians leaders often arrested on contrived charges

IN THE 21ST CENTURY...
The church will continue to be closely monitored by the government, and converts to Christianity will feel the full weight of social displeasure.

More than eighteen million people live in Yemen. They are overwhelmingly Arabs, belonging to some 1,700 clans or tribes, but there is a small minority of Somalis, Africans, Indians, and Pakistanis as well. Two-thirds live in rural settlements. Over half are under fifteen years old, and most will live to be fifty-five. While half of all adults are literate, three-quarters have no formal schooling at all. The population is growing rapidly and will likely double in just twenty years.

Yemen has a history fraught with warfare. Until 1990, the North and the South were politically two separate countries, although very much intertwined economically and culturally. North Yemen has been a feudal Muslim theocracy for more than a thousand years; South Yemen has been more open and has had substantial exposure to Christianity, though it still remains a very difficult area for Christian ministry. Even this dichotomy is simplistic; Yemen contains at least six distinct cultural areas including the Northern Tribes, the Mountain peoples, the Red Sea Coast, the Hadramaut, Aden, and the island of Suqutra.

Most workers are farmers, fishermen, or craftsmen, who supply goods to retailers in urban areas. There is almost no middle class; most are poor, but there is a small elite group of extremely wealthy people. Many farmers are growing qat trees, the leaves of which can be chewed as a mild narcotic.

The government is filled with war heroes and dominated by the rich. Military service is mandatory, and military bases pepper the countryside. The current president is a military hero from the civil war.

Islam is the official religion of the combined nation. The North is more conservative and desires the full implementation of shari'a law; the South is more moderate. More than 98.9 percent of all Yemenis are Muslims—most of the Sunni branch, with about a third from the Shi'a branch. A few Jews still reside in the country.

CHURCH LIFE

Yemen has traditionally been identified with the ancient biblical kingdom of Sheba. Many Christians lived in Yemen around A.D. 500, but were wiped out with the coming of Islam. There is a small minority of a few thousand Christians, but the majority are Catholic and Orthodox expatriate workers from such countries as Germany, Cuba, Russia, and the United States. Secret Yemeni believers number less than one thousand, many of whom have come to faith in Christ as a result of radio broadcasts, and who live in fear of what will happen should they be discovered.

PERSECUTION

The North has been governed by the Islamic shari'a law for centuries, and although it does not permit evangelism, it has been open in the past to compassionate relief ministries. South Yemen expelled all missionaries in 1973. No overt Christian mission work is permitted, and generally no permits are given for the construction of new churches. Some believers have been arrested, often on contrived charges, and imprisoned and tortured.

For Bilquis, learning more about Christianity has meant beatings from her own Muslim family. A friend says Bilquis discovered the Good News of Jesus when she heard a Christian broadcast on the radio. It touched her heart and she wanted to know more about Christianity. Against the odds, she found out there was a Christian near her home and began to study the Bible with her. But her Muslim family suspected she was interested in Christianity and beat her. Bilquis still meets with the Christian but she is terribly frightened; she knows if her family finds out, they will probably beat her again and put her under house arrest.

THE FUTURE

The church is growing, but slowly; it has added only a handful of believers yearly for the past century. And it is doubtful, under the current circumstances, that it will grow much beyond ten thousand this century, although many observers and workers believe a spiritual breakthrough is possible in the near future. Even then, the vast majority of Christians in Yemen will likely be expatriates; the number of indigenous Yemeni Christians will probably continue to be small, perhaps numbering ten to twenty thousand. The church in Yemen in 2050 will most likely be harshly persecuted and fearful for its very existence.

PRAYERS FOR THE SUFFERING

1. *The people suffer from spiritual darkness that almost completely blankets the land.* Islam has dominated Yemen for more than a thousand years. Pray for God to divinely pierce the darkness with the light of the gospel.

2. *Christians must use unique avenues to bring the gospel to Yemen.* Pray for the effectiveness of "tentmakers" (Christians who are in the land to work but have quiet, discreet opportunities for witness). Some have been able to share the gospel and make converts.

3. *Yemeni believers are cast out from the strong social structure.* Pray for Yemeni Christians to find one another in order to have fellowship. Christians in Islamic nations are often ostracized from a very close-knit social system; this can result in severe loneliness. The fellowship of believers—even in small numbers— can help to ease this situation.

4. *The only fellowship some converts have comes from Christian radio programs.* Shortwave radio broadcasts aimed at Yemen have been responsible

for hundreds of secret conversions. Pray for their ongoing success and for the development of successful methods for linking secret believers to other converts.

5. *Many Yemeni converts are completely alone in their faith while surrounded by Muslim loved ones.* They are married to Muslims and have Muslim children, and fear to share their faith with their family. Discovery could lead to arrest, imprisonment, and possibly death, but without anyone to fellowship with, many are in danger of retreating from their newfound relationship with Christ.

6. *Some Yemeni converts have been arrested and imprisoned.* Some of these have even been beaten and tortured. Many were arrested on contrived charges. Pray that the government will have mercy and release them, and for an improvement in relationships between Christians and the government.

7. *The leaders of Yemen lack a relationship with Jesus Christ.* Pray that the government will pass and honor laws that (1) guarantee religious freedom, and (2) provide for the free exercise of religion (particularly evangelism). Pray for Yemen's rulers to come to salvation.

APPENDIX OF WORLD RELIGIONS

ANIMISM Animism sees the physical world as interpenetrated by spiritual forces—both personal and impersonal—to the extent that objects carry spiritual significance and events have spiritual causes. Thus, if there is an accident, or if someone is sick, there are spiritual reasons behind such things that must be taken into consideration. The animistic form of a religion is called "folk religion," such as "folk Hinduism" or "folk Islam."

BAHA'ISM Baha'i is a recent world religion, dating to the middle 1800s. It claims to be the fulfillment of all other religions. Underlying principles include the oneness and equality of all people; the unity of all religions; and that truth is relative, not absolute.

BUDDHISM Buddhism began as a reform movement within Hinduism. Unlike Hinduism, it does not believe in a universal being or spirit, or that men and women have souls. There are three branches of Buddhism, but most Buddhists believe the four "Noble Truths": (1) Life consists of suffering—pain, misery, sorrow, and unfulfillment; (2) Everything is impermanent and ever-changing—Buddhists believe they suffer because they desire things that are worldly or impermanent; (3) The way to liberate oneself from suffering is by eliminating all desire; and (4) Desire can be eliminated by following an eight-point plan of right views, right aspirations, right behavior, right speech, right livelihood, right effort, right mindfulness, and right contemplation.

CONFUCIANISM Confucianism is more a system of ethics than a religion. It is based on the teachings of K'ung Fu-tzu, whose name was Latinized to Confucius by Christian missionaries. He was born and lived in China from 551–479 B.C.. Confucianism is concerned with a strong commitment to the family. It is founded on a strong moral ethic of practicing virtues, giving words of wisdom, doing good works, and having the attitudes of loyalty, trustworthiness, and respect.

Confucianism became the official "religion" of China, and remained such until the early 1900s. In recent years there has been a resurgence of Confucianism in East Asia.

HINDUISM Hindus believe that the human soul, called *atman*, is eternal and that it is linked with the universal soul or spirit, called *Brahman*, which sustains the universe. They believe that a person's social status and vocation is the result of his or her *karma*, or deeds. A person's karma determines the kind of body—whether human, animal, or insect—into which he or she will be reincarnated in the next lifetime. The chain is broken and salvation attained through knowledge, devotion, and good works. Unlike most other religions, Hinduism has no founder or set creed. It has temples but no established corporate worship or institutional form.

ISLAM Islam is the second largest religion in the world, trailing only Christianity. The term "Islam" means "submission" to the will of God, and the person who submits is called a "Muslim." The religion of Islam can be divided into beliefs and obligations. The central doctrine is that God is one and that no partner is associated with Him. It is a salvation-by-works religion, and each person has two angels assigned to him or her, one to record the person's good deeds and the other to record the bad deeds. Muslims are required to pray to God (*Allah*) five times a day. They are also expected to share their wealth to support the sick and needy. The amount of giving varies, but the practice is 2.5% of a person's income. Muslims, those old enough and in good health, are also supposed to fast from food and drink from sunup to sundown during the month of Ramadan (the ninth month of Islam's lunar calendar). Every Muslim, if possible, must also make the trip to Mecca at least once during his or her lifetime.

TAOISM Taoism (pronounced "*dow*ism") lies at the heart of the Chinese and Asian cultures. The religion/philosophy is concerned with achieving harmony with the universe. The three "jewels" of Taoism are compassion, moderation, and humility. When these three are practiced, and there is equilibrium between forces in nature, then there is harmony between humankind and the universe.

This appendix is adapted from Dean C. Halverson, *The Compact Guide to World Religions* (Minneapolis, Minn.: Bethany House Publishers, 1996); and John Schwarz, *The Compact Guide to the Christian Faith* (Minneapolis, Minn.: Bethany House Publishers, 1999).

LIST OF OPEN DOORS ADDRESSES

For updated prayer points, or to learn about additional resources and involvement opportunities with the Persecuted Church, please contact your national Open Doors office.

Open Doors
PO Box 53
Seaforth
New South Wales 2092
AUSTRALIA

Missao Portas Abertas
CP 45371
Vila Mariana
CEP 04010–970
Sao Paulo
BRAZIL

Open Doors
PO Box 597
Streetsville, ON
L5M 2C1
CANADA

Portes Ouvertes
BP 139
67833 TANNERIES
cedex (Strasbourg)
FRANCE

Porte Aperte
CP45
37063 Isola Della Scala, VR
ITALY

Open Doors
Hyerim Presbyterian
   Church
Street No. 403
Sungne 3-dong
Kandong-gu #134–033
Seoul
KOREA

Open Door
PO Box 47
3850 AA Ermelo
THE NETHERLANDS

Open Door
PO Box 27–630
Mt Roskill
Auckland 1030
NEW ZEALAND

Apne Dorer
Boks4698 Grim
N-4673 Kristiansand
NORWAY

Open Doors
PO Box 1573–1155
QCCPO Main
1100 Quezon City
PHILIPPINES

Open Doors
Raffles City Post Office
PO Box 150
SINGAPORE 911705

Open Doors
Box 990099
Kibler Park 2053
Johannesburg
SOUTH AFRICA

Portes Ouvertes
Case Postale 267
CH-1008 Prilly
Lausanne
SWITZERLAND

Open Doors
PO Box 6
Witney
Oxon 0X8 7SP
UNITED KINGDOM

Open Doors
PO Box 27001
Santa Ana, CA 92799
USA